The Once and
The Future Liturgy

J. D. Crichton

The Once and
The Future Liturgy

PAULIST PRESS
New York/Ramsey/Toronto

Nihil Obstat:
Richard Sherry, D.D.
Censor Deputatus.

Imprimatur
✠Dermot,
Archbishop of Dublin,
June 1977.

The *nihil obstat* and *imprimatur* are a declaration that a text is considered to
be free of doctrinal or moral error. They do not necessarily imply agreement
with opinions expressed by the author.

First published 1977 by
Veritas Publications,
7/8 Lower Abbey Street,
Dublin.

Library of Congress
Catalog Card Number: 78-61725

ISBN: 0-8091-2131-X

Published by Paulist Press
Editorial Office: 1865 Broadway, N.Y., N.Y. 10023
Business Office: 545 Island Road, Ramsey, N.J. 07446

Printed and bound in the
United States of America

Contents

1 Once.....

Once upon a time, they say, there was a fixed liturgy. This was decreed by the Council of Trent and carried out by Pius V who promulgated a revised breviary and missal (1568 and 1570 respectively) by his bulls *Quod a nobis* and *Quo primum* with stern injunctions that no one should use a liturgy other than those in these books unless their rite was two hundred years old or more. This "Tridentine rite" has been called a bulwark against Protestantism, a riposte to Luther, Calvin, Zwingli and, I suppose, Cranmer. Its doctrine is safe and sure; indeed it is one that must be maintained at all costs, otherwise the church will relapse into Protestantism and what is worse, Modernism. It was moreover drawn up *against* the heretics of the sixteenth century and *therefore* we can be sure that is is an equally powerful weapon against those in the Catholic church (including the pope) whose faith is now so obviously wavering.

Sometimes it is useful to carry out a little historical investigation when charges like these are made and one interesting fact that has been well enough known to liturgical scholars for a very long time is that the first printed missal of 1474, nearly a hundred years before the Council of Trent, differs hardly at all from the missal of Pius V. Apart from the rubrics, there are only three differences: the text of the *Orate fratres* is a little different, the *Placeat* is placed *after* the Blessing and said while the celebrant kisses the altar; there is no Last Gospel. Otherwise the text of the 1570 missal is identical with that of the 1474 one. It is difficult to see how a heresy could be refuted before it existed.

In fact the revisers had quite other considerations in mind. They were concerned to restore what they thought was the ancient rite of the Roman Mass and the pope in his bull says that they had consulted ancient codices in the Vatican library and elsewhere. Unhappily—and no blame to the revisers—they were unaware of the vast number of codices that have been the bedside reading of scholars for more than a hundred years and they were perforce ignorant of the historical scholarship on the liturgy which has come from the labours of scholars since the seventeenth century. Even the *Ordo Romanus primus* was hardly known until Mabillon published it towards the end of that century. What the revisers in fact did was to strip off a good deal (not all, alas) of the accretions that had come from Gaul and Germany during the Middle Ages. But it was not possible for them to restore the "original" Roman rite because it was then unknown. They did their best and produced an ordered version of the Romano-Germanico-Gallican rite.

In view of the blood-curdling threats that accompanied the promulgation of "new" books, it might be thought that the revision would be definitive. But no, things began to go wrong. Only thirty-four years later Clement VIII issued another edition. According to *his* bull there had been a certain tampering with the texts of his predecessor's edition. The Vulgate had undergone an inadequate revision and some had thought to replace the old pre-vulgate texts in, e.g. the introits, with the most up-to-date readings of the revised Vulgate. Clement is inclined to blame the printers but, anyway, he will have none of it and insists that his edition is now the definitive one and if anyone prints or sells a missal varying from his, he will be excommunicated, his press and books will be confiscated and he will be fined 500 gold ducats (though this last could only be levied in the Papal States).

This however was far from the end of the story. But thirty years later Urban VIII promulgated another edition of the missal and the breviary. He had a weakness for writing classical verse and some of it got into his edition of the breviary (e.g. the hymn for St Martina) but worse, he press-ganged four Jesuits into putting into a classical straitjacket all the hymns of the breviary. In his bull, after speaking of the recent work on the breviary, he makes the surprising statement that the "rubrics have gradually *degenerated* from the use and ancient rite". In some 60-odd years! He goes on relentlessly to say that he has ordered the missal to be "corrected". In what the "corrections" consisted it is a little difficult to say. Though papal bulls made a genuflection in the direction of literature—"the priest spreads his wings, as it were, before the Mercy Seat of the world by his use of the breviary and missal"—they are remarkably inexplicit and only a detailed comparison between the Pius V book (now only to be found in the greatest libraries) and that of Urban VIII would reveal the differences. But no matter. The details may have been few and small. What is important is that within a hundred years of the reform of the liturgical books by Pius V his successor is correcting them, changing the texts and straightening out, as he said, the rubrics. Like the bulls of Pius V and Clement VIII it is put out *Ad perpetuam rei memoriam* and, like them, ends with warnings, objurgations and sanctions against any one who dares to make a change.

What was the most striking change however was the addition of numerous saints' days to the calendar. A small matter, it may be thought, and inevitable if the church were not to look like a museum of sanctity. But it was directly against the intentions of Pius V and his revisers. They reduced the overflowing medieval calendars to 182 saints' days, including Marian feasts. The rest of the year was left free for the Masses of ferias, vigils, and of course Sundays, and it was the intention of the revisers that this should be so. They wanted the Sundays and the greater seasons of the year like Lent and Advent to be celebrated as they should be and, as far as the office was concerned, they wanted the psalter to be recited every week. Since "double" feasts made this impossible, they kept them to the minimum.[1]

Moreover the saints' calendar was very austere, consisting mostly of saints in the Roman calendar. They suppressed many and the irony of the situation is that Pius V's successors put them back: e.g. St Antony of Padua, St Francis of Paola, and the Presentation of the Blessed Virgin Mary. The multiplication of feasts went on remorselessly so that Mario Righetti could say that it all began *da capo*.[2] What the more immediate successors of Pius V began was continued to our times so that by the end of Pius XII's reign almost every day in the year had its feast and its celebration was only prevented by the rubrics and then only at certain times of the year.

All this may seem to be inevitable and a small enough matter in itself. The importance of it is that the successors of Pius V did not regard his missal and breviary as sacrosanct.

Various other, sometimes minor, changes took place in the course of the centuries. For instance, the use of the Preface of the Trinity was extended to all the Sundays after Epiphany and Pentecost in 1752.[3] But, alas, these Sundays were often impeded by saints' feasts and so could not be celebrated. In Lent, permission was given for the use of various votive Masses that could replace those of the season. As late as 1925, Pius XI instituted the Feast of Christ the King and put it on a Sunday where it still remains.

The reign of Leo XIII was a bad one for the liturgy. Numerous new feasts were added to the calendar, many votive Masses were permitted, and more baroque hymns got into the breviary. He *ordered* the rosary with other prayers to be said in October *during the Mass*—at least that was the effect of his legislation. He said in fact, *either* during exposition of the Blessed Sacrament *or*, failing that, at Mass, but since most churches could not have exposition daily, most of the clergy opted for the Mass. To add to the agony the prayers were kept on until 2nd November.

Then there is the curious story of the "Prayers after Mass" which came to be regarded as part of the rite. After 1870 Pius IX had become the voluntary "Prisoner of the Vatican". Leo hoped that this "imprisonment" would not continue indefinitely and he added certain prayers to the end of the Mass "For the Freedom of the Church". At first they consisted of three Hail Marys, the *Salve Regina*, and the collect of all the saints. Some three years later (1887), he replaced the collect with the prayer "O God our refuge and our strength" and added an invocation of St Michael. There the matter rested until Pius X added the invocations of the Sacred Heart. By any standards it was a curious amalgam and made the *Ite, missa est* irrelevant. Pius XI changed the intention to one "For Russia". By the 1950s people were getting a bit fed up with all this and the obligation to say the prayers was gradually relaxed. The New Code of Rubrics of 1960 does not mention them at all.

With Pius X came a phase of liturgical reform which was more various than is generally remembered. He not only attempted to reform church music and in fact promoted the restoration and use of the plainchant, but in the *Motu proprio* (1903) by which he urged these matters occurs the germinal phrase that active participation in the liturgy is the source of the Christian spirit. This was to have a long history which can be said to have reached fulfilment with Vatican II. It can be said to have changed people's attitude to the Mass. From seeming to be something that exclusively concerned the priest, it came to be seen as the action of the whole community. This, as is well known, was the main principle of the liturgical reform decreed by the Council. In addition Pius X, not a notorious progressive, dared to touch the sacred books. He completely changed the order of the psalter in the Divine Office. Whereas in the Pius V breviary "Mattins" could have as many as eighteen psalms, in the Pius X breviary the office never had more than nine. At the same time the 150 psalms were recited within the week. There were other changes of a more technical nature but all of them made necessary a new edition of the breviary which was very different from the old. The boldness of the pope's step has not always been appreciated. He changed the *ordo psallendi* that dated from before that of Benedict and that had been in use in the basilicas of Rome since the fifth century. Pius X had in mind a whole programme of liturgical reform for which he appointed a commission but other matters engaged his attention and it was not until 1920 that his successor, Benedict XV, was able to promulgate a revised missal which was necessary to bring it into harmony with the office. The reform of rubrics may seem a small matter but the effect of Pius X's new regulations was that Sunday Masses and those of the great seasons of the year could almost always be celebrated. He did much to restore the original appearance of the liturgical year.

Pius XII has often been described as a conservative pope but he brought about other and important changes in the liturgy. Of these the reform of all of the liturgy of Holy Week is the most striking. Here his commission not only wrote a complete codex of rubrics but they changed the pattern of the services and added new texts. The old *Missa sicca* for the blessing of palms was simply swept away. The Maundy was introduced into parish Masses, changes were made in the Good Friday service, and the "Mass of the Presanctified" became a simple communion service. The Easter Vigil was extensively re-ordered. These new rites were promulgated in 1955 and used for the first time in 1956. They meant a *radical* reformation of this part of the Pius V missal. Besides this, his extensive permissions to use the people's languages in the celebration of the sacraments, other than the eucharist, seem unimportant, yet pastorally they were of the highest importance and again they represented a departure from the *Rituale Romanum* of 1614.

Meanwhile things were happening at another level. There was of course the encyclical of 1947 which was described as the charter of the Liturgical Movement to which, even if it was somewhat cautious, it gave considerable impetus. There was, even during the war, the new Latin translation of the psalter which could and eventually did replace the "Gallican" psalter, revised by St Jerome in the fourth century and used in the West (Gaul, hence its name) from the seventh. One may suppose that St Jerome, if he knew about it, was not amused.[4] These various changes that had been made piecemeal had made the use of the liturgical books more and more difficult. There was the decree of 1955 *Simplifying the Rubrics of the Roman Missal and Breviary* and the New Code of Rubrics of 1960, already mentioned. This went a good deal further than the former document and the sum total of all these "simplifications" was to make the use of the current liturgical books even more difficult. A reform was imperative and was brought about by the Second Vatican Council.

Let it be said once again that the details do not matter. Nor is it for the moment a question of evaluating what has been done. It may have been done well or ill, it may have been wise or unwise to make the changes that have now been in use for so many years that few remember the old rite. The point is that throughout four centuries the popes have never felt bound by what their predecessors did. They have never thought, in spite of the *Ad perpetuam rei memoriam*, that they had their hands tied, and, equally forcefully, they have claimed the right to alter or reform the Roman liturgy. If what Paul VI with the backing of a general council has done is wrong, then all his predecessors were wrong, reaching back not merely to Pius V but to Innocent III, to Gregory VII, to Gregory the Great who added and subtracted things, to Vigilius, to Leo the Great, and beyond him probably to Damasus in the fourth century. What is not in question here is whether the popes have acted ill or well, or if it is a good thing or not to have a uniform liturgy in the Western Church. This is arguable and the French bishops at the Council of Trent argued it. They lost the argument and had their revenge more than a century later when they began editing and publishing their often attractive liturgical books. It can be argued today but that is not my concern for the moment. In the constitution of the church the pope has the authority to order its public worship. We may like the new church order, i.e. the liturgy as it now is, or we may not, but as members of that church we have an obligation to use it, unless permissions to use the so-called Tridentine rite are granted. They too depend on the authority of the pope. We may wish to change the church, and there are those who wish to change it back to what they imagine it was. If so, there are certain proper means for doing so, though those who would swim against the stream are in for some hard going.

What the "Old" Mass was like

Since there are many now, at least half a generation, who do not remember the rite before the Council, it may be useful to describe it and to set out the differences. We will deal with these first.

1. The penitential rite at the beginning of the Mass which existed since the thirteenth century in one form or another has undergone a slight change: the "I confess" shortened, alternatives suggested, and the versicles that follow it suppressed. With them has gone the psalm *Iudica* which in the former rite was frequently omitted, e.g. during Passiontide and at Masses for the Dead.

2. The Lectionary has been extended and at every Sunday Mass there has been added one extra reading and a responsor-

ial psalm which replaces the old gradual.

3. The offertory has undergone what seems at first sight to be considerable revision. The prayers speaking of the bread and wine as already consecrated have been replaced by others and the longish prayer addressed to the Trinity and giving the purposes for which the Mass is celebrated has been suppressed. The odd thing is that in the 1570 rite, excluding the prayers of incensation and the washing of the hands, there were seven offertory prayers. In the new rite there are six. Furthermore, it is interesting to learn that the commission set up while the Council of Trent was still in session (1562) questioned the propriety of the two prayers speaking of the bread and wine as the body and blood of Christ before they were. The Tridentinists are more tridentine than Trent.

4. The Roman Canon remains with three small changes: the insertion by Pope John during the session of Vatican II of the name of St Joseph into the sacrosanct list of saints that had not been touched for centuries; the addition from St Luke to the words over the bread ". . . which will be given up for you"; and the removal of the words *mysterium fidei* to the acclamation after the consecration. There are the three new eucharistic prayers which some have objected to because they do not express the sacrificial nature of the eucharist clearly enough. A mere reading of Eucharistic Prayers III and IV shows that this is just not true. The second is based on the prayer of Hippolytus, c. 215, and *he* was a conservative. If the objection is urged that it does not contain the *word* sacrifice, one wonders whether some are desirous of indulging in mere logomachy. In any case the eucharist is called "sacrifice" three times during the offertory act.

5. The changes from the *Pater noster* onwards are slight, hardly more than a straightening out of the rubrics.

A Matter of Celebration

One wonders what all the pother is about. It looks as if it is all a matter of celebration. The rite remains intact but there are many ways of handling *both* the old and the new rite.

One of the ironical features of the old rite was that it was rarely if ever celebrated according to the rubrics of the Pius

V missal. If you pointed out that the celebrant should mark the missal in the sacristy before Mass and that it should be carried out by the server, you were unpopular. If you drew attention to the rubrics requiring that a third candle should be lit at the *Sanctus* or that the altar should be dressed with an antipendium, i.e. frontal, you were regarded as a rubrical purist. If you suggested that certain texts of the Mass like the epistle and gospel should, according to the rubrics, be said audibly, you were regarded as a fussy martinet. One could lengthen the list without difficulty. In fact there was a widespread and long-standing disregard of many of the Pius V rubrics and one of the most constant complaints some twenty five years ago was that priests celebrated Mass so badly. It was inaudible, it was hurried, and those that wished to "follow the Mass" in their missals were unable to do so.

This, then, was what the Sunday low Mass was like. The celebrant, preceded by one or two servers approached the altar, genuflected, gave his biretta (a black cap made of cardboard and cashmere) to the server on his right. The priest then ascended to the altar, arranged the chalice, went to the right and opened the book. He descended and began the psalm *Iudica*, went on to the confession, gave the absolution, recited some versicles and responses, said two prayers as he re-mounted the steps and went to his right-hand corner where he read the introit (entrance chant) and the *Kyries*. He came to the middle to say the *Gloria*, turned round to say *Dominus vobiscum* and then went to the right to say the collect, the epistle, the gradual (or tract) and the *Alleluias* with the verse. The server than moved the book to the left-hand corner of the altar to which the celebrant moved to say the gospel. On Sundays, in most places (though not in all) he went to the pulpit (or altar-rail) where he read the announcements, the epistle and gospel in the language of the people, and preached (but not always). He then returned to the altar, said the Creed, and performed the offertory, offering the bread, pouring the wine and water, etc. This done, he turned to the people and said *Orate, fratres*, said the "secret" prayer and went on to the preface (in principle to be said audibly) and the Canon which had to be said inaudibly. Bells rang at the *Sanctus* and the Canon proceeded in silence. The host and chalice were raised after each consecration when the bells rang again. The *Pater noster* was said (again in principle audibly) to be followed by the *Agnus Dei* and other prayers before communion. The celebrant communicated himself and the servers said the "I confess" again and then he turned towards the people and gave another absolution. He then opened the tabernacle, took out the ciborium, turned to the people, held up a host and said *Ecce, Agnus Dei* and the rest. The people approached the altar rail and received communion in one kind alone—always. After the communion act the celebrant cleaned the chalice, went to the right-hand corner of the altar, said the postcommunion prayer, came to the middle, said *Ite, missa est*, gave the blessing, then went to the left hand corner, recited the "Last Gospel" (*John 1:1-14*), knelt in the middle of the altar-steps, and said the Leonine prayers (in the people's language). This done, he took the chalice from the altar, descended, genuflected with the servers, put on his hat and went to the sacristy.

This is but a brief description of the Mass as it was celebrated until 1965, for a long time and in most places. That it could have been celebrated in a different way and in fact was, is shown by the prevalence of the "Dialogue Mass" in use in Europe and in many English-speaking churches from the late 1920s onwards. This revealed what had for long been forgotten that the Mass, even of the Pius V missal, was an action of the community, a point that Pius XII, in his encyclical *Mediator Dei*, was concerned to illustrate from the rite as it then was and with some help from that eminently Tridentine theologian, St Robert Bellarmine. Celebrated in this way the rite looked and was very different and yet not a single rubric was infringed though some pernickety persons questioned the legality of the procedure, basing themselves on particular interpretation of *"circumstantes"*. Were they those in the nave or those "standing around" the celebrant in the sanctuary?

On the other hand, the present rite could be celebrated much as the old without infringing any existing positive law. Thus the celebrant could turn his back on the people if he wished, he could of course say the whole Mass in Latin, a server could make the responses and so on.[5]

There is experience to show that when the rite of 1970 is

thus celebrated most people are unaware of the differences from the old rite. One has only to put the matter like this to see how bizarre a procedure it would be. If no law is broken, the celebrant would be going against the entire spirit of the Second Vatican Council. He would almost certainly be in trouble with his bishop who would point out to him that the Mass is for the good of the people not for the preservation of certain traditions.

2 The Future and the Liturgy

The first question of course is whether there will be a future to have the liturgy in. The signs of the times are not encouraging. World bankruptcy in the midst of plenty seems to be a possibility and that may lead to the breakdown of public order. Countries and whole regions would in those circumstances disintegrate and anarchy would ensue. New power groups would emerge and they might well be ideologically hostile to Christianity or indeed to any form of religion. The process, already observable, of the decline of the humanist tradition by which Europe and other parts of the world have lived, would bring its extinction. Men would not reason; they would shout slogans at each other. They will not listen to reason; they would knock down the man who opposed them. Science, which is based on the principles of reason, would become impossible and the technology which depends on it would cease. Before that happened there is the possibility of the destruction of large parts, if not the whole, of the human race by an international nuclear war. Even if that did not come about, we have to assume that the consumer-waste system that is current will continue and life will have less meaning for millions than it has now. These things are possible though they are mercifully or unmercifully hidden from our eyes.

On a more optimistic view, however, the run-down of our present civilisation may bring advantages. If the present power-groups, whether within nations or among them, were to break down, if social life received a different orientation, there might well be opportunities to re-think the meaning of life and room for the insertion of the gospel message. The bureaucratic organisation of life, whether it is based on governments, on business, commerce or industry, makes personal and social life difficult and sometimes impossible. It is now a platitude to say that people are suffering from the anonymity of modern life and vast numbers wish for something different. Many are looking for a change, though they hardly know what they are looking for. Nor, for that matter, do others, least of all the writer.

It is not difficult to see that the decline and fall of the present order would in many ways impoverish life and bring suffering in its train. Much that has made life tolerable for the old, the young, the sick, the handicapped would no longer be available and the amenities of life that we take for granted, like quick though no longer cheap transport, would fade away. What Christians may *not* do is to adopt a *philosophie du pire* and *desire* the downfall of our way of life. If we were willing to accept suffering for ourselves (and how few of us are?) we have no right to impose it on others or even to wish to do so. None the less we may "redeem the time" and use what falls to us for the presentation of the gospel. If society lost something of the imposed uniformity that is characteristic of it, it would mean that it would be broken up into smaller groups, the impersonality people complain of would at least be mitigated and the witness and work of small Christian groups would be more evident.

This in turn suggests that a re-structuring of the church will be necessary if it is to make the gospel present and effective where human beings are and live. For the church also has suffered from the trends and fashions of our time. Its centralising tendencies grew particularly from 1870 and they can be said to have begun far back in the eleventh century with the Hildebrandine reform, but one effect of which was the virtual demise of the Mozarabic liturgy in Spain. Vatican II has changed the emphasis, though whether it has changed the direction is another matter. It puts emphasis on the local church (the diocese or a group of dioceses) and local conferences of bishops have a great deal more freedom to manage their own affairs than they once had. The introduction of vernaculars into the liturgy has inevitably meant a certain regionalism in the church. Language is not just a noise: it is the vehicle of a whole culture and the cultural differences from region to region in the church are now much more apparent than they have been for hundreds of years. It is slowly, too slowly, becoming apparent too that it is not uniformity, organisation and law that hold the church together but a common faith and a shared love.

But if decentralisation is taking place in the church, the impression given by the Roman curia is that it must be checked and strictly controlled. The observer may too easily gather the impression that there are those at the centre who only very reluctantly accept the present situation and are fearful of the future. If we are to judge by what is being done, or not done, or by what is only unwillingly allowed, there is a mood about that suggests regression. What the post-Vatican II church has granted with one hand is being taken back with another. A rite for the communal reconciliation and absolution of penitents is granted by the Order of Penance but its use is apparently being inhibited in practice. Theological manuals made beautiful bonfires after the council and now, we are told, are to be brought back. Three "agreed" statements of the Anglican-Roman Catholic International commission have been issued but there has been no single official comment on any of them. A statement on the question of the ordination of women is issued by the Congregation for the Doctrine of the Faith—and one has no quarrel with that—but it would appear that that body never consulted the Secretariat for Christian Unity in spite of the fact that the ecumenical implications of the question are both obvious and acute.[1]

If these factors mark a trend, in ten years time we shall be back with the Tridentine Mass in Latin and the inter-sectarian warfare that was regarded as necessary to maintain the identity of the One True Church. No doubt all this will give great satisfaction to those who until 1962 could be described as *beati possidentes*. The church was theirs and now they are unhappily dispossessed. However a warning light has appeared that should daunt those who, like the perishing Egyptians, cry "Back, back" when it is far too late. There would not be one but a whole army of Lefebres-in-reverse who, like so many but more successful Canutes, would bid the waves of reaction recede.

Be that as it may (and it may not be as I think), if the church is to move into a new age, it needs a spirit of adventure, a boldness in proclaiming the gospel, like the apostles, and a willingness to forgo anything that hampers the mission of the church. The Vatican Council announced very clearly that it was the servant, the *diakonos*, of the world in which it perforce exists. But if it is to be so, it must see that this is not just an admirable sentiment but one that needs to be carried through to the details of its organisation. For a Catholic it is unthinkable that local churches, however rich in genius and culture, should even wish for an autonomy that would be the contradiction of Catholicity. The church in Eastern Europe is well aware of the strength that comes from its relationship with the papacy. In its measure that is true of every region and the one thing we should fear is a *national* Catholicism. To want that is to confuse nationality with culture. Given this strong attachment to the centre, the centre itself needs confidence, first in itself and in its ability to adapt readily to new situations, and then in the local churches which are concerned to make the church with its gospel present to men and women wherever they are to be found. All of us, however, must have confidence in the church which we believe to be guided by the Holy Spirit.

But are there grounds for that confidence? There are two ways of considering a predicament, two ways of looking at a future that seems to indicate the obsolescence of much in the church we regard as necessary. We can see it as an almost unrelieved calamity, as the breakdown of the church. Populations dwindling, congregations shrinking, the number of priests diminishing, debts mounting, buildings deteriorating and any other form of ruin the jeremiahs like to turn their minds to. On the other hand we can see an emergent situation as a *kairos*, a privileged moment, in which God may be revealing to us the direction in which we should go. We may, and should, see that the work of the church, the proclamation of the gospel and the bringing of people to God by word and sacrament, can be done in a variety of ways. It will be possible to discover new truths about the church, to see it in a new way. Vatican II gave us a new vision of the church, that is, it set out that vision in broad lines. It gave a sketch-plan. It is for us to fill in the details. Its main insight was that the church is the People of God and among other things that the role of the people in the life of the church is a central and essential one. This needs translating into practice. Parish councils, area pastoral councils, national pastoral councils are on the way but so far and in most places they have no responsibility for what is done. That is still the prerogative of the clergy. But we have to ask: is this an eternally decreed law? Why should not the parish, for instance, be a "moral person" (in the terms of English law) that carries the responsibility for the community, for its planning, for decisions about what is to be built or if anything is to be built, how it is to be paid for, and, without infringing on the priest's strictly sacramental role, how the liturgy of the parish is to be organised? The answers to such questions would undoubtedly clarify the role of the priest in the parish community and the chances are that he would be more effective in such a situation than he has been in the past. In a word, if certain features of church life are giving rise to anxiety, the positive way of dealing with them is to see them as so many questions posed to us. If we, if the church, is willing to face up to them, and in the process to come up with difficult and perhaps unpleasant answers, that will be the moment when we shall be able to make decisions. We shall begin to see what must be done if the word is to be proclaimed and the liturgy celebrated. What is pretty certain is that if the church is unwilling to adapt to new situations, neither will be done.

There are other questions of course. Should celibacy as a condition of ordination to the priesthood be abolished in the western church? Should married men be ordained? Should women be ordained? Is it tolerable that there should be a plurality of theologies in the church? These are all ecclesiastical and mostly intra-mural questions with which the "world" is not preoccupied and all must be reviewed and examined in the light of the indispensable mission of the church to carry the saving word of God to all mankind. Only then shall we find solutions.

Meanwhile we must address our minds to the question of the liturgy and this will involve some treatment of it as it now is and some indications of what it will be in the future.

3 The Future of English

Until recently, language has been regarded as the principal means of communication and one wonders whether this is still so. For one thing, the signs are that we are entering an age of illiteracy. This of course will be nothing new as, in the whole history of the human race, the age of universal literacy, never completely achieved to this day, has been a very short one. The odd thing in our own time is that though most people learn the techniques of reading, they use them rarely enough. The visual image is replacing the word and the spoken word is being drowned in noise. People deliberately create noise. They fill silence with the sounds that come from television, and the radio, and transistors are everywhere. The cocktail partly, long a symbol of our "social" life and which has been described as an expense of spirit in a waste of shame, is an occasion when no one can hear what anyone else is saying and it is usually not worth it if you can. Perhaps the new age should be described as that of "inaudibility". Like Caliban's island, it will be full of noises that will not only be incomprehensible but no one will listen to them. Is it possible that in the future, near or far, we shall have a Mass so overlaid with noise that the congregation will be able to do no more than watch it? If so, it will be a case of *plus ça change, plus c'est la meme chose*—like that Mass I celebrated at Pourville on a hot Sunday in September 1937 when a section of the Paris Conservatoire obliterated the Mass with the exquisite music of a string quintet. If the ways of God are inscrutible, the ways of man are too various to be comprehended. No doubt there will be those making a case for the "Mass of Noise". They will want an "experience". If the noises were sufficiently varied—on present showing they would have to be of the "thumpity-thump" kind—and if there was a suffi-

cient exploitation of lights with colours, they would have
their experience of the psychedelic sort—as it was called some
time ago. But, ineluctably, noise would bring other consequences. The sacred drama would have to be dramatic, if
while the ears were filled with noise, the eye was to get
satisfaction. A single celebrant, however elegant and expert,
would act in vain if the attention of the people was to be
held for, say, thirty minutes. So with noise would come
movement involving a number of "players" who would act
out the meaning of the no-longer-heard texts. Every Mass
would have to be choreographed and tricked out with lights
and various kinds of electronic devices. It would become a
rare, and rarely performed experience and the Sunday obligation would wither away. All things are possible but not all
things are probable and however improbable the above
picture it should remain with us as a cautionary tale. If the
word is devalued we are leaving the door open to every kind
of lunacy.

Meanwhile there is the immediate problem of the English
language. It has become, we are told in Latin, the *lingua
franca* of the world and, like Greek in the centuries immediately before Christ and like Latin in the first Christian
centuries, it is going to take on new forms, new idioms and
will form new words that are unknown to us now, as indeed
many already in existence are to those of us who are verging
on seventy. Already the links with Latin which via Norman-
French had so great an influence on the formation of our
language have become tenuous. If you read a speech of Glad-
stone's, you would think you were reading Cicero. If you
read the first few pages of Scott's *Waverley* you would be
strongly reminded of Livy. Contemporary English eschews
the dependent clause wherever it can. It has adopted a para-
tactic syle, rather like Hebrew: it puts one statement after
another and the reader is required to find the consequenti-
ality of the one from the other, always supposing there is
any. The adverb is becoming a casualty: e.g. we hear that
someone has taken up some work or other on "a voluntary
basis", that is voluntarily. Almost everything is done nowadays on a "basis" even if there is nothing to stand on. Adjec-

tives have become sterotyped: e.g. if someone who has had
an interesting experience is interviewed on TV and asked what
it was like, you can bet that the answer will be "fantastic";
though it will usually have no connection at all with fantasy,
that precious gift. People's active vocabulary is shrinking all
the time, that is, their ability to find a sufficiency of words
to describe what they know or have seen or heard is much
less than it used to be. The passive vocabulary is also shrinking. In my experience people are understanding fewer and
fewer words, those that have formed the very stuff of the
English language, although some know a great many technical
terms that are part of their trade or profession. Scientists,
particularly, have coined, for good or for ill, thousands of
words and terms that are known only to the initiate. To the
uninitiate like myself they are not only incomprehensible,
they are unspellable and unpronounceable.

There is a similar impoverishment of religious language.
This should not be thought surprising since we live in an
irreligious age. This is so fundamental a matter that we find it
difficult to communicate even our notions of God to an age
that does not believe in him. If you say that "Father" is a
basic Christian word for "God", as it is, someone is sure to
come back at you and say "from my experience 'father' is
the last word I should wish to use of God". Alternatively,
you are liable to be called a "male chauvinist pig" for daring
to think that God is masculine. "Gentle Jesus, meek and
mild" has been mocked out of existence, yet he *was* gentle
and meek, if we understand that word, as well as other
things. One could lengthen the list: "incarnation", "redemption", "grace" and many other words have become non-con-
ductors. But most probably it is devotional language that has
undergone the greatest devaluation. A phrase like "Most
loving Lord, Jesus", apart from its alliteration, is no longer
acceptable to most people, at least in public worship. But I
think it is the adjectives that have become most unacceptable.
In the language that was traditional, it is not unfair to say
that no noun could exist without its adjective or perhaps two
or sometimes three. Everything had to be "holy", "sacred"
or even "pious", a word that could be used apparently without qualms a hundred years ago but not now. "Almighty"

and "Blessed" became inseparably attached to "God" and
"Lord". No doubt all these words and many others witness
to deep devotion of our forefathers, though I think it would
be true to say that by the time my generation had inherited
them; they had become no more than irritant *clichés*. It is
difficult to make clear without quotation what this language
was really like and I will illustrate what I mean by a prayer
that dates from the mid-nineteenth century, which I copy
from the official *Manual of Prayers* dated 1936, though the
imprimatur is 1921 and the letter of approval by the English
hierarchy headed by Cardinal Manning bears the date 1886.
This prayer is still, as far as I know, ordered for the second
Sunday of the month whenever there is Benediction:

> O most loving Lord Jesus, who when thou wert hanging on the
> cross, didst commend us all in the person of thy disciple John to
> thy most sweet Mother... May her sweet name be lisped by
> little ones, and linger on the lips of the aged and the dying; and
> may it be invoked by the afflicted, and hymned by the joyful;
> that this Star of the Sea being their protection and their guide, all
> may come to the harbour of eternal salvation.

There is I think no need for extended commentary. We
merely note "O most loving Lord Jesus", "thy sweet mother"
and "sweet name", the string of inevitable adjectives. We go
on to wonder at the strange request that children should be
made to lisp and at what seems to be a necessary feature of
this language, namely alliteration with a certain amount of
unconscious assonance: "May her sweet named be *lisped* by
little ones, and *linger* on the *lips* of the aged and the dying..."
The prose, too, aspires to the condition of verse which all the
critics say it should not do. I do not know what the impact
of this would be on modern people nurtured on a more
vigorous prose but we cannot help but notice that the adjectives are such as we should not wish to use today.

Let us set beside this another prayer which comes in a text
to be found in the *Divine Office:*

> Grant us, Lord, your help and protection. Deliver the afflicted,
> pity the lowly, raise the fallen, reveal yourself to the needy, heal
> the sick, and bring home the wandering people. Feed the hungry,
> ransom the captive, support the weak, comfort the fainthearted.
> let all the nations of the earth know that you alone are God, that
> Jesus Christ is your Child, and that we are your people and the
> sheep of your pasture.

This I submit is a vigorous prayer which could be used by anyone today, even the fastidious. Perhaps we should prefer to say "discouraged" for "fainthearted", though that is an exact translation of the original, but we also note, apart from "wandering" which is necessary for the sense, there is not a single adjective in the whole passage. Yet this prayer was written in Greek by St Clement of Rome towards the end of the first century, A.D.. Which only shows we do not need "pious" adjectives to make good prayers.[1]

What, if anything, has all this to teach us and what of the future? The first observation to be made is that we still have a translated rather than a truly vernacular liturgy, and it is difficult to believe that we shall ever have at our disposal people of sufficient genius to make a translated liturgy read like native English. It is not just a question of turning words, however skilfully, from Latin into English. Liturgical Latin belongs to a different world. The literary forms and style of the Roman liturgy, especially in its older strata, owed much to the Greco-Roman civilisation in which it was formed and the language was often a cult-language that derived from pre-Christian times as well as the Christian era.[2] This is particularly evident in the Roman canon, the older prefaces, the collects, the prayers over the offerings (i.e. *orationes supra oblata*) and the post-communion prayers. The word *"Clementissime"* in the canon probably owes as much to Byzantine court ceremonial as to the Christian notion of God. A little lower down is a series of cult words: *"haec dona, haec munera, haec sancta sacrificia illibata"*. There is here a rhythm, repeated constantly throughout the canon, and a vocabulary that would have evoked all sorts of associations in the mind of the fifth century worshipper for whom pagan sacrifices were the memory of but yesterday. Even if they can be translated in tolerable fashion, they have no resonance for the twentieth-century Christian. This is not to say that the Roman canon should be abandoned but it does mean that the wind has to be tempered to shorn lambs and the ICEL translators should not be taken to task for doing so. *"Clementissime"* has been dropped and *"haec dona. . . "* has been telescoped without the loss of anything of real value to present-day Christians.

A similar difficulty is found with the collects. When translating a collect, you first have to look for the sense and then you find that usually it is embedded in a certain amount of religious rhetoric which is there on account of the rhythmical system, the *cursus*, that largely dictated the pattern. You have to strip this off, because even if it is good rhetoric it is not *our* rhetoric, and then sometimes you find that there is little enough left. This is one reason why the *ICEL* collects sometimes seem so stark.

It is unlikely that a translated liturgy will give satisfaction for very long though should we abandon the Latin texts altogether. The prospect is not encouraging. We have come but recently to a vernacular liturgy and have yet to learn how to say what we want to say, always supposing we know what we want to say. Then there is the heavy heritage of the devotional language of the nineteenth century. Whether *as a community* we are willing to abandon it is not clear. If at present we were allowed to ignore the Latin texts and make up our own, I am not confident that the results would be better. But there is something that is far more important. Sooner or later we shall be faced with the need to create our own liturgical language, a language that will express the faith, the religious sentiments, the mentality of English-speaking Christians. It will have to be a language that emerges from our way of thinking and doing things, as did the Latin that was the language of the Roman rite for sixteen hundred years. What this will be like cannot, I think, be foreseen at the moment. Cultural considerations will have their influence and that is one reason why we should be concerned about the apparent decline of English. But a sense of community, of what community worship needs and demands, will be of equal importance. The language that is suitable for private devotion or for the devotional service outside the liturgy is not suitable for the public worship of a Christian community.[3]

This however is not to go to the root of the problem. We have inherited from the Latin liturgy not only certain ways of addressing God but certain literary forms and we must consider one of two of these now.

4 Literary Genres and their Future

It is not always realised that the liturgy contains a great variety of literary genres or forms. There is prose and poetry, there are statements and cries (acclamations), there are lyrical pieces and more prosaic ones, there are prayers of exultation and prayers of supplication. All these and more existed in the Latin liturgy and were strongly moulded by the Latin language. There is the rhetorical roll of the ancient prefaces, there is the peculiar rhythm of the Vulgate, comparable to that of the Authorised Version, which had so strongly formative an influence on the composition of the Roman liturgy, and there is the complicated form of the collect which was constructed according to certain rules that were native to the Latin language. In fact, the one feature common to all these forms is their Latin linguistic form.[1] It hardly needs saying that these forms are far removed from the genius of the English language and are becoming more so as English is moving steadily away from its Latin links. But what perhaps has not been sufficiently observed is that Latin was a rhetorical language. It was one that fell easily into certain patterns and conveyed its message partly through those patterns. When a prayer began *"Omnipotens aeterne Deus"* the mind could rest on the strong rhythms announcing a truth about God. Another could begin very strongly *"Protector in te sperantium Deus, sine quo nihil est validum, nihil sanctum"* and the mind was not only held by this proclamation of God's nature and man's relationship to him but the message of the prayer was equally compelling, driven home in the concluding petition *"ut, te rectore, te duce, sic transeamus per bona temporalia ut non amittamus aeterna."* The pattern enforced the message. Such was the nature of Latin; the literary form was consubstantial with it. We can only guess at these things

29

but it seems fair to say that the people could "latch on" to
the prayer and make it their own. In spite of Miss Christine
Mohrmann's view that the stylised Latin of the liturgy in the
fifth century was far removed from the language of the ordinary people, it is difficult to suppose that they could not
understand *"ut. . . transeamus per bona temporalia ut non
amittamus aeterna."* There is not a single "difficult" word
there and the rhythm gives it what one can only call a
"punch-line".[2]

The same I think could be said of the Easter Vigil *Exultet*,
one of the finest rhetorical pieces of the Roman liturgy (for
all that it was composed outside Rome!). Here, the people
would be carried along by the beauty of the language and of
the chant and might well have had only a general sense of its
meaning. But both words and music come out of a particular
culture and were the artistic expressions of it and while you
can transfer words from one language to another with more
or less success, you cannot "translate" a whole cultural
expression. The result is rather like an English translation of
Virgil. In other words, texts like these could say something to
people of that culture because it was part of their culture and
they were attuned to it, whether or no they were particularly
"literary" or even literate.

This brings us to a consideration of the literary form of the
collect. The collect was probably the creation of fifth-century
Rome—St Leo's sermons are full of collect phrases—and it
must be described as hieratic, the prayer of the pontiff at an
impressive ceremony in a vast basilica. He visibly and audibly
presided. It is not without interest, too, that it was called
oratio, a word that suggested both discourse and, for the
Christian, prayer.[3] Perhaps it would not be unfair to say that
it combined rhetoric with prayer. It was a particular art-form
and at its classical best had a comparatively short life. The
form deteriorated through the centuries until we arrive at the
baroque collect of the seventeenth and subsequent centuries
when it had become wordy and shapeless. It too, then, was
the product of a particular culture that has now passed
away and one wonders whether even in translation, and a
good translation at that, it *says* anything to the modern
Christian.[4] Or, what is more important, does it enable the

modern worshipper to *pray*, that is to lift his heart and mind to God? Even when it is said slowly and with due attention to the sense lines, the people seem to have a glassy look in their eyes, and when it is uttered as quickly as possible, as, alas, is still the case in some places, one wonders what either celebrant or people make of it at all. Is it just something to be said because it is in the book? Or does it work in some peculiar *ex opere operato* way: it is said, *tant bien que mal*, and something happens in the celestial spheres? But even granted it is said as it should be, does it add up to prayer *for the people*? If my suspicions are correct, it does not, and it may well not have a very long future before it.

There is in fact an important principle at stake. The collect is indeed a presidential prayer and it belongs to the president to lead it. But does that mean he must monopolise it? On the other hand, there is the principle, basic to the new Order of the Mass, that the people must have their full part in the celebration and that participation is at the level of prayer/personal commitment, and not mere noise. If this is being taken seriously—and it seems to be taken rather more seriously by the laity than by the clergy—we shall, I think, hear demands for a greater part in what, after the eucharistic prayer, is the most important prayer of the Mass-liturgy. We need then to see if there is another form for this prayer that would preserve both the presidential role of the celebrant and allow a greater participation by the people.

There is in fact a very ancient form of prayer, going back to the fourth century, which might well give us a clue. We are familiar with the form from the Good Friday liturgy and it seems to have been the model of the Anglican *Series III* for the intercessions. As will be remembered, there is an invitatory, sometimes quite full, of the "intention" that is the subject of the prayer, there is a pause for silence, and then the prayer is summed up by the celebrant. The people make response first by silence and then by *Amen*. Both priest and people are involved though the involvement of the people does not seem to be very great. But at least their thoughts are directed, they are invited to pray and after due preparation they have time to make a meaningful assent. There would seem to be no reason why this pattern should not be taken as

a model for future prayers of the community and indeed the
ICEL translators have already moved in this direction. They
have extended the invitatory *"Oremus"* of the Latin missal
with a phrase indicating the subject of the prayer. This cor-
responds to the first part of the *oratio sollemnis*. But what
one is looking for—and what I believe many people are looking for—is a greater scope to take part in the prayer itself. If
this is to be made possible, it will of course mean that the
shape and style of the collect will have to be changed. Experience shows that there is need for this from a linguistic point
of view. The predominant grammatical mood of the Latin
collect is necessarily the subjunctive. That is how Latin
works. Yet in English the subjunctive is gradually becoming
obsolete and when you try to turn a Latin subjunctive into
English "May he. . . may we. . ." the effect is somewhat
weak. In collaborating on the translation of the collects of
the *Divine Office*, I noticed that whenever it was possible to
use an imperative for the Latin subjunctive one got a much
more vigorous result. Here is an example: "Lord God, deepen
our faith, strengthen our hope, enkindle our love, and so that
we may obtain your promise, make us love what you command".[5] The Latin, it is true, lends itself easily to such treatment: it has two imperatives (*da* and *fac*) where the English
has four and in both there is but one subjunctive but coming
in the English after a "so that" it has a certain strength.

Another prayer that begins with two subjunctives in the
Latin goes easily into one imperative in English for its first
clause: "Lord God, open our hearts to your grace. Let it go
before us and be with us, that we may always be intent upon
doing your will".[6]

These two samples, and others could be cited, suggest that
the imperative in English is often the real equivalent of the
Latin subjunctive. It also appears that it would not be difficult, nor I think inelegant, to construct a prayer from a series
of imperatives to which the people could reply in the course
of the prayer. Thus in the first example above a response of
the people such as "Hear us, Lord" could be inserted after
the first three petitions. The subjunctive clause would of
course end in the usual way with the response "Amen".
Entirely new prayers could of course be longer and admit of

more than one response of the people. The result would be that the people would be actually praying while the prayer was being *said*. This is surely desirable and, given a new form of prayer, not difficult to achieve.

The postcommunion prayer is another that could well benefit from similar treatment. Especially in the *ICEL* translation they are usually too brief for the people to make much of them, and often somewhat jejune in content. In fact the conclusion of the Mass has come in for criticism for some time. There are those who say it is too abrupt and does not provide sufficient opportunity for thanksgiving. The last sentiment should be treated with caution. There *is* time for thanksgiving either by the silence that is to be observed or by the hymn that is to be sung and the purpose of the postcommunion prayer is not thanksgiving but the appropriation of the fruits of communion and indeed of the whole eucharist which *is* thanksgiving.[7] The pattern suggested above could very well spell out various aspects of the eucharist and of the liturgical year, as the blessings do, with phrases for the people who would then be able to appropriate to themselves the fruits of the eucharist.

The one place where some such device seems to be particularly necessary is of course the eucharistic prayer itself. Traditionally it is all but a monologue and one wonders what the people make of it *as prayer*. Are they just listening to someone reading it? Are they reading it at the same time as the celebrant and if so, is such a reading prayer? One purpose of the eucharistic prayer is to enable the worshippers to offer themselves, to join with Christ in offering their lives and work. Mere listening and mere reading are not sufficient. Can we envisage a different pattern?

1. First it should be observed that there are *three* interventions of the people in the current rite: at the *Sanctus*, after the consecration, and at the end.

2. The principle of further interventions has been already admitted. These are to be found in the three eucharistic prayers provided for children's Masses. In the second formula there are no less than twelve, though oddly enough the acclamation after the consecration is omitted.[8]

3. In the *Order for Infant Baptism* there are two altern-

atives for the blessing of the font in each of which there are repeated interventions of the people. Thus: "Praise to you, almighty God and Father, for you have created water to cleanse and give life"; to this the people reply "Blessed be God" or, as the rubric says, "some other suitable acclamation". But the prayer for the blessing of the water has always been in the form of a eucharistic prayer in the broad sense. It is a prayer of praise and thanksgiving followed by petitions and the invocation of the Holy Spirit.

It is obviously not revolutionary then to suggest that this form of prayer should be extended. It seems to be what many are looking for. No doubt considerable skill is needed to make a good prayer but it should not be beyond the wit of man. In addition, the second formula for children's Masses has pointed up a simple but necessary device: there must be a "cue" said by the celebrant to "lead in" the people. If adopted, the form would draw the people into the central action of the eucharist and at the same time would not detract from the presidential role of the celebrating priest.

Another peculiarity of the Roman prayer is, as is well known, the absence of an epiclesis or invocation of the Holy Spirit. Yet this may not always have been so. The Roman canon certainly underwent some re-writing in the fifth century and it is not wholly improbable that in the course of it an epiclesis disappeared. There is a phrase of Pope Gelasius (died 496) that seems to indicate the presence of an epiclesis: *"Quomodo ad divini mysterii consecrationem coelestis Spiritus adveniet. . .".*[9] In the same century though from Africa (the links between Rome and Africa were always close) there is a statement of Fulgentius (died 527 or 533) which is worth repeating: *"Cum ergo S. Spiritus, ad sanctificandum totius Ecclesiae sacrificium, postulatur adventus, nihil aliud postulari mihi videtur nisi ut per gratiam spiritalem in corpore Christi, quod est Ecclesia, caritatis indisrupta servetur".*[10] This is a good example of what might be called the western epiclesis. It does not ask for consecration or change for the elements but for the sanctification of the sacrifice and for the fruits of holy communion, that is the charity that makes the church one. We recall too that in the Gallican liturgy, eighth century, and usually in the Mozarabic liturgy there is an epiclesis of the Holy Spirit though its presence is sometimes explained by eastern influences.[11] That may be so but one is also impressed by the basic Roman-ness of much of the Spanish liturgy.

Whatever weight is to be attributed to this fragmentary evidence, the revisers of the Mass-liturgy since the Council decided not to touch the Roman canon. But, as everyone knows, they have added not one but two epicleses to the new eucharistic prayers, the first, deriving from the Alexandrian tradition, asking that the elements may become the body and blood of Christ, and the second that the Holy Spirit will come upon the assembly so that they may be one in Christ and make a fruitful communion. This, without attempting to decide whether the epiclesis of the Holy Spirit is a theological necessity or whether it is consecratory in the eucharistic prayer, is a recognition that it is a practical necessity. As a recent writer has put it: since "it belongs to the nature of man to give some expression to his deepest beliefs and feelings or to risk having them stagnate" an explicit epiclesis of the Holy Spirit is practically necessary.[12]

In the light of the foregoing it seems reasonable to conclude that the eastern pattern of the eucharistic prayer is the more satisfactory one. It begins with *eucharistia* and continues to recall it in its recording of the words of God in creation and saving history and to this the *Sanctus* appears naturally as the response.[13] This in turn is attached to the next part of the prayer which leads to the words of institution and continues with the *anamnesis*, the invocation of the Holy Spirit and concludes with the doxology. This is a coherent pattern and it is broadly that of the fourth eucharistic prayer prayer that is based on an eastern model.

But to the liturgical pattern must be added a basic theological pattern which in fact underlies all eucharistic prayers with the exception of one or two that must be described as eccentric.[14] Invariably the eucharistic prayer is addressed to the Father, the thanksgiving and offering are made through the Son, who appears in his central priestly-mediatorial role, and concludes by invoking the operation of the Holy Spirit. This pattern is not only essential for a right understanding of the eucharist and for the maintenance of the right balance

in its various elements but it is also essential for a right understanding of the Christian faith itself. Any eucharistic prayer
of the future will have to be built on this fundamental pattern.
So much for pattern. What about content? By this I mean
the theology that is implied by a prayer and the language in
which it is expressed. The new missal contains a considerable
number of prefaces to the eucharistic prayer and many of
them are new compositions. Yet not only is the language
traditional but the thought behind them is that of an age that
has passed away. As I have said elsewhere (and I include the
eucharistic prayers as well): "One feels that if the revisers had
been in close contact with modern thought and life they
would hardly have produced prayers like these" and "the impression given to the sharp-minded young is that of a *Weltanschauung* that is no longer credible."[15]

There is a Sunday preface (V) that is good, especially in its
teaching that man is the steward of creation, but the implica-
tion is that God made all things rather as he is recorded as
doing in Genesis I. The young ask, "How? In the twinkling of
an eye? In Six Days?" as one boy, when told the creation
story, said, "I can't make sense of it. The scientists
say. . . ." and he had to be given a mini-lecture on literary
forms. Again, if man has a vicarious function in relation to
created things, how far does his writ run? Does God interfere?
"All things are of your making, all times and seasons obey
your laws" as the preface goes, and we know that there is a
sense in which this is true, but does it not suggest that God is
immediately responsible for rain or lack of it, for thunder-
storms that kill people, for floods that drown them? We cannot, I think, afford to go on giving wrong impressions even in
liturgical prayers and especially liturgical prayers. *Lex orandi,
lex credendi!*

What we shall need, what we need already, are prayers that
show an awareness of the creative process as we now understand it, a gradual process which is a complexus of secondary
causes and one in which man is ultimately the collaborator
with God.[16] We need prayers that are sensitive to the ways
modern man thinks of the universe in all its magnitude,
variety and almost limitless possibilities, prayers that give
thanks for the work of man in science, in technology and in

all the ingenuity he shows in exploring this infinitely varied world. Yet another dimension of these prayers should be the expression of the concern that men and women of today feel for each other throughout the inhabited world, which to borrow a well-worn phrase, has long been a global village. In a word, the prayers need to express something of the world as man knows and experiences it today. It is this world that has to be lifted up to God, it is this world that needs to be reconciled and redeemed by the saving power of Christ, it is this world that needs to be permeated by the Holy Spirit.

Nor would this be a real innovation. While the Roman texts, whether ancient or modern, show little enough concern for the created universe, this is not true of some eastern liturgies, e.g. that of St Mark.[17] They show a considerable awareness of the creative activity of God, they exult in the things he has made, which are a manifestation of his greatness and beauty, and by sharp contrast they point up the "humiliation" of Christ in incarnation and passion. It is true that the language is traditional, because biblical, but the roots of the matter are there even if we see that there has to be a radical translation at the level of thought and theology.

Such a transformation will also involve a transformation of language in which such prayers would be expressed. This is obviously a problem but since language is the expression of thought, with the right kind of thinking comes the language in which to express it. The Roman liturgy was nourished on the Vulgate, though not exclusively, and the Greek liturgies on the Septuagint, but both owed something to the language of the church councils.[18] That is, they were able to absorb and transform this language so that it could become a medium of prayer. If that was once possible, there would seem to be no reason why the same process should not take place in our own time. The Greek definitions of Nicaea and Chalcedon seemed to many at the time too remote from the biblical, semitic world to be acceptable but this language won the day even if it is now under critical review. What the new language will be like it is difficult to say but it is clear that new prayers will have to be composed by those who are familiar with the thought of our time and move within it with ease. It is improbable therefore that the writers of new prayers will be exclusively ecclesiastics.

There is another problem. Would it mean that the eucharistic prayer would be constantly changing? The answer is yes and no. If man gets new insights into the nature of the universe and the social and political organisation of human life, it would seem that these insights should be expressed in the prayer. But since even now man's *Weltanschauung* changes slowly, it will not be necessary to change the text of the prayer with any great frequency. But there is another issue here. It is not perhaps sufficiently realised that when people ask for change, it is not the basic patterns of the liturgy that need changing but the language that clothes them. The pattern of the eucharistic prayer will remain fixed but the possibility should always be left open that texts can be changed. Of this we speak elsewhere.

5 Adaptation: The Way to the Future

If it is agreed that the liturgy has a future, it must be asked not merely what direction it should take but on what principles, if any, it should be based. Is it to be by way of free and uninformed "experimentation", or by an equally baseless innovation? Is one suggesting that it would be a free-for-all in which the fittest, however judged, are to be the survivors? There have been manifestations in the church which seem to suggest that all three might be tried but in fact the seeds of development will be found in the work of the Second Vatican Council and in that of the Congregation for Worship.

A feature of the 1960s, after the Vatican Council had decreed a reform of the liturgy, was an outbreak of liturgies that were called "experimental". What these experiments consisted of is a little difficult to discover as for the most part they were composed (if that is the right word) in the "underground" church that flourished in the United States and elsewhere. A little of it did surface and one has heard accounts of a "liturgy" that consisted of the reading of a passage from the Bible (rather conservative that) chosen at random, some sporadic remarks shared by the president (in lay dress) and his audience, some sort of *ex tempore* eucharistic prayer which ended with communion given to all who ranged from Buddhists to Roman Catholics. In Holland, the paradise of the progressives and the target of the conservatives, there was a plethora of eucharistic prayers, thirty-two at one time, though I understand that this was a gross underestimate. It is alleged that no difference was made between the consecrated bread (of course leavened) and that which was not consecrated. The readings were as likely to be from a modern communist as from the Bible. Other places had other "happenings" and at one time it looked as if there was not so much experimentation as anarchy. All this was of course grist to the conservatives' mill and every time the pope or the bishops have insisted on the obligation to use the rite of 1970, the conservatives have pointed to the unauthorised goings-on of the left. The simple truth that two wrongs do not make a right seems to have escaped them and apparently they have not realised that their call for the forcible suppression of these experiments rebounds on their own heads.

One is naturally prompted to ask why this happened, why people who had hitherto not manifested any interest in the liturgy and were usually grossly ignorant of its meaning and history, should have launched out on a campaign of liturgy-making the like of which has not been seen before. One explanation must be that since the Second Vatican Council and the papal actions that followed it relaxed a certain number of rules that had been rigidly insisted on up to that time, there were those who could not take the new freedom without becoming intoxicated. It is perhaps significant that the two countries where liturgical libertarianism was most prevalent, the United States and Holland, before the Council had been among the most law-abiding in the church. Indeed, the impression one got of the church in America before the Council was that it was held together by a rigid system of canon law. What was not law was not anything. Nor can it be irrelevant to the situation that most of the American bishops had come up through the chancery and saw everything through the eyes of the law and had no pastoral experience into the bargain. The liturgy requires a certain knowledge of theology and if this was always true, it is even more true since the council for the Constitution on the Liturgy is basically a theological document. But if a liturgy is to be successful its use requires pastoral experience and knowledge of people. However deep its theological foundations, it exists only in the order of action and as the Constitution, as well as the missal of 1970, makes very clear the liturgy is celebrated *by* the people with the ordained president. The liturgy does not exist in the abstract nor is it confined to the black or red print of the book. That is no more than a libretto.

There is however another reason that is more likely to engage our sympathy. We have lived into an age when life is

largely unstructured or rather one where structures and habits
are *imposed* by impersonal forces, whether governments or
industry, and when people can wriggle out of that area of
life, by way of reaction they evade fixed patterns of living as
much as possible. Ours is also an informal age and for good or
for ill the *mores* of a former time which provided certain
safeguards for, say, expressions of emotion, and certain
structures for daily living that made social life more tranquil,
have gone. The young at least are much less inhibited in
matters of love and sex, and for that matter in those of
violence, and in the satisfaction of their needs, real or imagin-
ary. In verbal communication the high-sounding phrase, anything that smacks of rhetoric, turns them off. Yet the
"manners" of even the current liturgy are formal, the pattern
is fixed, one event leads to another, certain formulas that
accompany the actions are for the most part also fixed. It
may be (though who can be certain of it?) that it is this style
of worship that is unacceptable to a great number of the
young and the not-so-young who think like them. They may
well be seeking a less formal kind of liturgy in which they
could be more at their ease, a liturgy that would say something to them as they are. An attempt to deal with this
matter will be made later.

Meanwhile it is perhaps necessary to recall that adaptation
has been written into the Constitution on the Liturgy and, at
least in a limited way, into the texts of the liturgy itself. The
matter is treated at some length (37-40) and if the perspective seems to be "missionary", its statements cannot be limited to that. Not only are almost all countries "missionary"
nowadays but the world is in rapid evolution and what may
have been appropriate in 1963 may be so no longer. In the
nature of the case, the adaptation spoken of in the Constitution must look towards the future and since it was promulgated in 1963 there has been a certain amount of development, this time official. When the first part of the Mass was
turned into the vernaculars of various countries and regions,
it was seen soon enough that the Canon would have to be
said aloud though still in Latin. This was granted and then
that was seen to be anomalous too. So it was translated and
at the same time alternative eucharistic prayers were written

and put into use in 1968. This was a development that was probably not foreseen by the fathers of the council though it was implied by the Constitution (n. 34). In the middle sixties when "folk music" was first used at Mass, there were some bishops who banned it. Now, for better or for worse, it is common enough and raises no eyebrows though understandably some dislike it. In the same period when the first essays in liturgical translations were being made it was assumed that the style should be more or less traditional (the "thou-thee-ers" fought a hard but losing battle), rather like the "vernacular" translations of the hand-missals which many used. Two documents on the subject were issued by the Congregation for Worship giving the translators considerable freedom and this they have used. In the ICEL translations that are now official we have versions *based* on the Latin but that are distinctly adaptations—to the dismay and sometimes fury of those who write to the Catholic press. The alternative collects they have provided for the Sunday Masses are even more remote from the Latin and are to all intents and purposes new creations. This is not to say they are always successful.[1]

Although liturgical art and architecture were developing rapidly before the council, the development has continued in a way that was hardly conceivable before 1962. The new churches undoubtedly look new, in shape and form, and the talents of modern and untraditionalist artists have been used for their furnishing and decoration. Not all that has been done has been well done. One thinks of those famous circular churches that are not at all adapted for liturgical worship and of the sometimes unhappy re-orderings of old churches whose character has not been respected. But we live in an imperfect world, and in a period of change mistakes are inevitable. Even in periods when men were working in a well known tradition, as the Middle Ages, there were mistakes: towers fell down, nave did not meet chancel where it should, and pillars were not always secure enough to support the roof. Carvings were sometimes less than perfect and Nottingham was almost a factory of mass-produced alabaster altars, reredoses and statues.

Vestments too have taken on shapes that would probably have been banned in 1950 and chalices and other altar plate, some of it *kitsch*, look very different from what they used to. To balance this there has been a sort of new puritanism that has made the interiors of some new churches very stark. But whatever we may think, there has been a considerable change in just over a decade and this means that in some respects the church has been moving into the future all the time. That there should also have been jolts and hesitancies is not surprising and it is to be hoped that they are not typical of the period that lies ahead of us.

Geographically speaking there have been changes outside Europe that may be harbingers of the future. In Africa, Mass vestments are in the style of the local art — and why should they not be! But many seek a much more radical thinking that will lead to the use of African attitudes and gestures in worship, indeed to the making of an African liturgy. It has been reported that in some regions of Africa there is a tendency to look towards eastern rather than western models for a liturgy that will be adapted to the African mentality. If so, it should produce some interesting results that should be useful to us. We might be tempted to repeat *semper aliquid novi ex Africa*. May it be so! In India, certain adaptations are being made: e.g the "peace" is given in the Hindu manner, as the pope did on his visit to the sub-continent and, as it seems, gave great satisfaction to vast numbers of non-Christians.

The question is whether the present situation is supposed to be the end of adaptation. There is a *vis inertiae* in human nature that always holds a people back. There are those who hate to think the world is moving on, whether it does so with or without them. There are those who think that the church reached the peak of perfection at the Council of Trent. There are others who used to think that all that was medieval was beyond questioning. Some have said that the present liturgical reform is harking back to the "classical" liturgy of the seventh century. But whatever period in the past has been regarded as the "perfect" Christian age, it has inevitably gone. The church cannot go back to *anything* unless it is to die of suffocation. We may and should go back to the past to discern primitive patterns in the liturgy; they may reveal factors we have forgotten, they may show up the organic lines or forms of Christian worship, but we may not *imitate* what was done in the past. The church is a living body, it is and must be concerned with people living here and now. In the course of centuries its vitality has been so great that it has been able to incorporate and use the language, the gestures, the actions and the music of contemporary cultures. But always in the history of the church there comes a time for stripping. Sometimes, most frequently, it is done by the world. Sometimes the church takes the initiative and it is to the credit of the church of our age that it has done so. That there were values in the past that are of more than ephemeral worth is undeniable but they must be *used* as and when possible and not allowed to dominate. The demise of the Latin language in European civilisation is undoubtedly a cultural loss and unless we are to relapse into a chronological parochialism, it must be revived. But given that the whole trend of society is against it, that represents a herculean task. And even if there were a revival, that would not justify a liturgy in a language that is not our own. "Knowing Latin" (to O level?), to be able to contrue a passage of Virgil or Cicero is one thing; to be able to pray in it, to feel at home in it and to be able to cope with the complexities of the Vulgate, is another. To cling to a past cultural element of our worship is really an attitude of despair.

The statements of the Constitution imply that we should look at our contemporary cultures and see what is valuable in them. The trouble is that the industrialised world does not seem to have a culture or if it has, it is one that seems hostile to Christianity in general and worship in particular. In this the peoples of Africa, India and no doubt elsewhere are more fortunate. Theirs are cultures that are still related to human living or rather are embedded in it. Their elements are various, ranging from ceremonial forms of greeting to natural rites that emerge from the rhythm of nature. "The rites of passage", birth, growth, marriage, and death are still realities and call for sacramental celebrations whether in the narrower or broader sense. In our culture they barely survive. Birth is clinical, growth is either a bore (to the parents) or a licence to misbehave (for the young); marriage is giving way to cohabitation which may be terminated at the will of the partners; and death, at least until very recently, is taboo. Language is becoming corrupt all the time, declining into a series of noises, and communication, that much vaunted quality of our time, is gradually ceasing. England has probably produced more great poetry than any other nation and yet there is now no poet who appeals to a wide cross-section of the people. The immense richness of the English language is being eroded and the verbal associations, the assonances and the rhythms that not only nourished the poets but made their work pleasurable to their readers, are no longer known. Music is in a more flourishing condition but if we wanted to look for a truly "folk" music that might be of some use to the liturgy, where should we go? The various forms of "popular" music that have swept the West since the war are the folk music of someone else and their erotic rhythms are hardly suitable for worship. Of the visual arts it can be said we have made some use and this has transformed the appearance of our churches.

Then there is the difficult question of symbols. The liturgy exists in the world of symbols and where the sacraments are concerned they are essential to it.[2] Bread, wine, water, oil, the laying-on of hands are constituent elements of different sacraments. Yet our age seems to be a very *unsymbolic* one. People look for what "works", for what is useful and above all for what will make money. To call this view materialistic is both a platitude and a denigration of matter in which lies a potential of beauty that goes far beyond utilitarian purposes. There is of course beauty in a finely designed machine operating so harmoniously that would be breath-taking if we stopped for a moment to reflect on the matter. It is indeed a right use of material things but, alas, it seems infinitely remote from the symbolism of worship. That example perhaps indicates that there are *two* worlds, the world of efficiency and the world of symbols that creates no material value. Seen like this the two may well exist side by side but one should not exclude or seek to dominate the other. What has happened in fact is that our scientific and technological civilisation has formed a mentality that finds it difficult to enter the world of symbol. Yet attempts to do without them have been short-lived and futile. When the heirs of the *philosophes*, those very cerebral characters, threw out the Christian religion at the time of the French Revolution, they had to institute the Feast of Reason. But they could not do without symbols and on the high altar of Notre Dame they set up a "temple", flanked by busts of Voltaire and Rousseau, from which the "Goddess of Reason", played by an actress of dubious morals, emerged. When the icy-minded, "sea-green" incorruptible Robespierre replaced her with his *Être Suprême* he had to have his symbol: Atheism was burnt in effigy. Quite a feat. But it was the only celebration. Nearer our own time, communists are said to have invented a rite of "confirmation" though it seems to have had no future.

Oddly enough that experiment may put us on the right way. Man cannot *create* symbols. He can only find them. They are rooted in nature, in the basic things and experiences of human life: bread, wine and water are all necessities of human living as are the handshake, the embrace and the kiss. If there are more conventional signs, like the laying-on of hands, they too have emerged from the consciousness of man who sees that certain ways of doing things are inherently appropriate. To surrender symbols then would be to de-humanise man and that may well be the source of much of the modern malaise. Further, if we look at the great symbols of the liturgy we find that all of them are related to human living, to a way of life that was indeed simpler but that was literally down to earth. They have come from the ways of living of people in the Old and the New Testaments and have, one would dare to say, an eternal validity. If this is so, the church must retain them and do all that is possible to enhance their importance. But, alas, even Christians have been affected by the *Zeitgeist*. In practice, symbols are too often *not* seen to be important. A smudge of anonymous oil, stilted and truncated gestures, scrambled ceremonial, are all signs that symbols are disregarded. If there is one thing that is to be done in the future it is that the value of symbols must be a primary concern not merely at the level of intellectual discussion (there is a whole new science of signs, semiology) but at the level of practice. The Easter Vigil is often a jejune affair because the richness of the symbols is neither explored nor exploited. That is the line along which we must go; we must make the most of what exists and in so doing we shall discover values that are hidden in the symbols that are already in the liturgy.

We should then look forward to eucharists where real bread is used, where it is normal practice that the people should receive in both kinds, to the restoration at least on occasions of baptism by immersion, to baptism and confirmations when the oil is abundant and sending throughout the church a fragrant odour, to celebrations where the gestures are meaningful and generous, and where time and space are enlisted to make services both tranquil and joyful. The remedy in other words is not fewer symbols but the better use of those we have got. If as a result, a celebration should verge on the dramatic, we should not be dismayed. If the people of our day are starved of symbols, perhaps the only way to inculcate their need is to use them to the maximum of their potential. Where the inhibited victims of industrialism are concerned there is a little danger of excess. If on the other hand there are symbols that of themselves are non-significant we should be willing to surrender them forthwith. The anointing before the act of baptism is almost certainly one of these.[3] And since the use of oil in many parts of the world is a difficult symbol, because it is not closely related to the life of ordinary people, we should be willing to forego its use unless it is necessary to the integrity of the sacrament. Anointings in ordinations are no more than "explicative rites" and *could* be dispensed with. This is probably true of confirmation which in the second century seems to have been administered by the laying-on of hands and without anointing.[4] The *law* of the eastern and western churches is that the administration should be done by anointing but this could be changed. In fact, the only sacrament to which anointing is essential is that of the sick and here the church has permitted the use of vegetable oils other than that of the olive (Order, 20). This is an example of adaptation making possible the use of substances that are regional or local in places where olive oil is unknown.

Lying behind this however is the principle that the church is bound by the New Testament and this means that she has no power to abolish the symbols that are essential to certain sacraments. On the other hand, there is nothing to prevent the church from extending the use of symbols and of adopting them from cultures where they are meaningful. We may not be very enthusiastic about the origins of the anointings in ordinations—the transference of the custom of the anointing of monarchs in the tenth century to bishops and then priests—but they were speaking symbols at the time and did something to enhance the dignity of the priesthood at a time when this was necessary.

The problem before us is complex. Symbols of their nature must be self-explanatory or they are nothing. Hence if certain symbols do not speak to people they should be dispensed with. But may it not be necessary to enquire *why* they do not speak to certain people? In the industrial West it seems likely that the sensibility of people is becoming atrophied; the trends of modern life, the pressures that are upon them, are slowly dehumanising them. If this is so, then there is a case for the church retaining symbols that seem to be obsolete and waiting until the pattern and style of life changes so that they once again become credible. But the principles stated above remain valid. Whether it is a question of retaining certain symbols or of providing what might seem to be new ones they must be related to human living and be in some way extensions of the great symbols that are to be found in the Bible. In the Middle Ages the Mass suffered from a heaping up of "symbols" that were in fact acted allegories: all those signs of the cross in the canon both before and after the consecration, the multiplication of genuflexions and bowings and the rest. That sort of thing must remain a cautionary tale for posterity.

We return to the question of a less formal kind of liturgy. Those who want this may not remember the rigid ritual of pre-conciliar days. Then the celebrant's gestures were rigidly regimented, they were manifold, they were supposed to be absolutely uniform (but of course were not in practice) the world over wherever the Roman rite was used, and some of them were meaningless. Thus, the position of the hands out straight with the elbows touching the body and the palms facing each other had no meaning whatsoever. It was a piece of rubrical drill, a travesty of the ancient *Orante* position which presumably had been forgotten or was regarded as old-fashioned, something of interest to archaeologists only. Bodily attitudes, positions, places to be in at a particular moment, were all strictly regulated. Even the garments worn, the stiff sandwich-like vestments, the strange square hat (mostly of cardboard covered with black material), all chimed in with this system of rigidity and uniformity. The effect on the observer in a large church was that of a marionette being pulled by wires. Useless however to recall these things to people who have never seen them, vain to suggest that the ritual of the current liturgy is or can be more flowing and easier in movement. They still want something more shirt-sleeve like. Or do they? Do they know what they want? Do they really want celebrants in short jacket and trousers or servers in jeans and sweat-shirts with their favourite football team written all over them? Some sort of garment that conceals the unpredictable bulges and anfractuosities of young or more ancient human bodies is surely a charity to those who are inevitably and to a certain extent observers. Are they willing to forego all ceremony? Do they see the point of ceremony? It is first just good manners; secondly, necessary for the right conduct of any function, secular or religious; and thirdly, and at best, can convey something of the meaning of the rite. Even to modern people arms outstretched are a sign of welcome, the handclasp a sign of friendship, and the raising of the hands a sign of supplication.

However it may be readily admitted that gestures and ceremonial are adaptable to different circumstances and of course should be. What is "right" in a large church is not right in a small church, where one can be more relaxed, and is contra-indicated for the house-group where the setting is that of a family. The requirement of one of the Instructions in the period before the missal of 1970 that Mass-vestments, the lot, must be worn on such occasions was not very intelligent. Vestments, especially if they are heavy with gold lace and "decorated" with ecclesiastical "symbols" worked out by some church furnisher, are simply incongruous in such a setting. In a word, adaptation applies here too, and what is required is a bit of common-sense and a spot of imagination.

But we need to think about the matter along rather different lines. If a liturgy, any sort of liturgy, is to be comprehensible, if it is to be usable by a miscellaneous body of people (and such are Christians), it must have a predictable form, a sense of direction, a beginning, a climax, and a conclusion. Perhaps this truth was obscured for Roman Catholics for they knew only two services: the rigid rite of the 1570 missal and the ritual rag-bag that did duty for evening "devotions". The first could not be varied anyway (not even the pope, according to some) so you had to put up with it, and, to the second, people became inured for reasons that were less apparent. Neither however really made sense. In churches where neither the epistle or the gospel were ever read in the vernacular many could not distinguish between the ministry of the word and the ministry of the eucharist, and the pious regarded the Mass as a prolonged preparation for communion which was the only moment that interested them. The Roman liturgy, like every other liturgy, has always had a comprehensible pattern and its revelation in practice has dismayed some people. It has consisted of a ministry of the word, readings from scripture, punctuated by a psalm and other texts, a homily, prayers of intercession, a presentation of the gifts (more or less elaborate in different ages), a eucharistic prayer and the act of communion. These are the basic elements of a Christian eucharist and it is difficult to see how any of them could be dispensed with.[5]

These then must remain but perhaps it needs emphasising that it is *structure* that is permanent and all else can be varied. The *way* they are handled need not in *principle* be rigidly laid down, though it is a protection for the people that it should be. There could be fewer or more readings (as there are on occasion), the psalm could be sung in unison throughout if the community were capable of it, the intercessions can and do take a variety of forms, some good some bad. The "offertory" can be reduced to the simple act of placing the bread and wine on the altar, as they were in the time of Justin (c. 150 AD). Even communion admits of a variety of practices: people can kneel or stand, they can receive in one kind or both, they can receive by intinction or from the chalice through a reed, and all these practices, except possibly the last, are in use. We may well envisage a liturgy in the future when the liberties allowed for by the present rite and others that grow out of it will be reduced to practice and the rite will be less rigid.

But if the broad structure of the liturgy must remain, does it follow that the same must be said of the *texts*? Although there is a much greater variety and therefore choice of texts in the current liturgy, I suspect that the ground of complaint is to be found in this area. We say something about texts elsewhere; here we are concerned with the impact of constantly repreated texts on the community. In worship it is so easy to recite parrot-fashion texts that occur every Sunday and for the clergy every day. This leads to precisely that quasi-mechanical performance of liturgy that the council was concerned to bring to an end. The matter of a greater variety of texts and fewer fixed onces becomes peculiarly acute and delicate where the eucharistic prayer is concerned. The provision of three new ones has undoubtedly alleviated the situation though the fourth is limited in use by rather strict rubrics. It may not be used on the greater occasions of the year, when it would often be appropriate, if there is a "proper" preface. The question then has been asked: is it necessary always to have fixed, written texts, or even is it desirable? The answer is a matter of some delicacy not only because of the need to preserve orthodoxy (and here again the people deserve protection from the caprices of local celebrants) but because a eucharistic prayer is a text of a special literary genre. Here again, I think, it will be as well to make the distinction between structure and text, in this case between the structure of the prayer and the language it might be couched in.

If we look at the great eucharistic prayers, that may in some sense be called classical, it is possible to establish their fundamental elements and the order in which they occur:

1. There is the calling of the divine names (God, Lord, Father, Almighty, Creator...) which derives from Jewish usage and is a way of ascribing praise and thanksgiving.

2. There follows a recalling of the works of salvation at greater or lesser length.

3. These are said to be effected "through Christ our Lord", the Mediator.

4. This proclamation leads to the first response of the people, the *Sanctus*.

5. There is usually then a reference, longer or shorter, to

the works of salvation leading to:

6. The words of institution accompanied or followed by an acclamation, the second response of the people.

7. Then comes the *anamnesis*, the celebration, recalling and making present the principal redeeming acts of Christ, passion, resurrection, ascension and (usually) reference to the Second Coming. This is combined with praise, thanks and offering.

8. The epiclesis of the Holy Spirit follows.

9. The whole prayer is concluded with a doxology leading to the third response of the people, *Amen.*

Within this pattern there are some variations, e.g. an epiclesis of the Holy Spirit before the consecration, but in broad lines it is the basis on which any such prayer must be built.

If this is clearly seen then it should be possible to create prayers in which not every word is written down but which would always preserve the basic pattern. In other words, there could be considerable *verbal* variation within the prayer that would make it adaptable to particular needs, circumstances and occasions. Given an understanding of the structure of the prayer, it would be possible for the celebrant, in consultation with his colleagues and his people, to write a prayer that would be appropriate and perhaps called for by the occasion. This in turn would affect the *style* in which it was written. It would be easier, the language of the group, perhaps almost conversational, and would thus meet the request of those who look for a less formal liturgy.

Nor would there be anything really new in this. As is well known the first eucharistic prayers were *ex tempore*. This is clear from Justin the Martyr: the president (*proestōs*) "sends up" prayers and thanksgiving "to the best of his ability" which would seem to indicate that some were more "able" than others.[6] The famous prayer of Hippolytus is a *model* for the newly ordained bishop and not necessarily to be followed *verbatim*. Later, when local councils were held they concern- ed themselves with the eucharistic prayer but it is interesting to note that the Council of Carthage of 397 was concerned with the trinitarian *theology* of the prayer which must always be addressed to the Father.[7] Even in the case of the Roman rite there were a number of texts circulating before the Roman canon received its definitive form somewhere about the middle of the sixth century, and the Mozarabic rite to this day witnesses to an earlier tradition when there were "movable" parts of the eucharistic prayer.[8] Like modern people the Spaniards, and the people of Gaul for that matter, felt that the Roman canon needed variation.

Of course there are dangers in such a procedure. Not only is the business of composing a eucharistic prayer peculiarly difficult, calling for special skills, but there is the danger of theological deviation which has been shown to be real in our own time. But it should not be difficult to set up a reasonable system of control. If a local conference of bishops authorised an agreed structure in which all the necessary elements of the prayer were laid out, it should not be impossible for others, the clergy in consultation with their people, to compose the text or texts. They might well not be of high literary merit but then neither has every prayer that has in the course of time achieved the dignity of publication been a model of literary elegance. Nor should it be thought that such prayers were being composed for ever and for aye. Their precise value is that they speak to people in particular circumstances and at a particular time. The *libelli missarum* that in the fifth and sixth centuries were composed *ad hoc* were often not very impressive as pieces of Latin prose and although many were "filed" to become the sacramentaries, we may guess that much was rejected. If even this amount of control were thought to be insufficient it would be at least possible to lay down that certain texts, edited by a central authority, should be used but space could be left for insertions to be made by the celebrant or members of the local church.[9] This would be particularly appropriate for the intercessory part of the eucharistic prayer that comes after the second epiclesis and which is not an integral part of it.

The conclusion then is that our liturgy could, while retaining its basic shape, be much more flexible and allow a degree of adaptation that is proving to be necessary if we are to have a liturgy that is alive, that speaks to the people, that involves them not merely in "participation" in the sense that they say something, but would draw them into prayer and lift them up to God whose praises they are gathered to sing.

6 The Mass of the Future

Father Gerald Ellard, S.J., published in 1948, a book entitled *The Mass of the Future* which was regarded as mildly revolutionary in its time, largely on account of the last section which gave the title to the book.[1] Chapter-headings like "Latin-Gravitation Neutralised" and "Streamlining for the Age of Air" (though he omitted to mention the nuclear bomb) did nothing to mitigate the wrath of the conservatives. Much that he asked for was granted by the Second Vatican Council and a good deal more than he hoped for. Perhaps we may take it that excursions into the future are made not entirely in vain.

In recent years the Mass has been at the centre of contention and in the newspaper controversies that have raged through the press of the Catholic world other parts of the liturgy have gone unscathed. It is curious that it should be so. Does it mean that the Catholic people are familiar with the Mass alone? Does it mean that anything may be changed and they remain unruffled but that when the Mass-liturgy is changed they feel that the very foundations of the church have been moved? We must leave the answers to those possessed of the gift of discernment of spirits. To some extent of course the phenomenon is understandable. In the pre-conciliar church people were too often brought up on rigid notions that they took for dogmas and that at best were sometimes no more than half-truths. "The Mass is the same everywhere"; and of course it wasn't. Millions of Catholics "heard Mass" in rites that were different from the Roman. "Latin is the universal language of the church"; and of course it wasn't. Those same Catholics heard their liturgies in a variety of languages ranging from Ge'ez to modern Arabic. The abreactions of some people since the council is a symptom of the extreme westernisation of the church that is by definition Catholic and too many were victims of that situation. In a word, it was not their fault.

Objection to changes in worship is however a very common phenomenon and since the Mass *was* the most familiar form of service it is not surprising that people were disturbed. Change of ritual patterns, whether secular or sacred, whether those of childhood or adult social life, breeds insecurity and people do not like feeling insecure. When it is sacred ritual that is in question people feel outraged because the deepest springs of their relationship with God seem to be touched. Though a good deal of what has been said in recent years about the "sacred" and the "numinous" is questionable when applied to Christian worship, it is in fact an indefinable quality that is attached to all that we mean by worship. But there are those who have wanted to put the emphasis in the wrong place. They have spoken of the sacred quality of the "silent" low Mass apparently unaware that such Masses were always infringements of the rubrics. They have pointed to their experience of the numinous at High Masses when what was moving them was not the sacred reality of the Mass but the sounds and lights and movements that went to make up its ceremonial. But these are changeable and through the centuries have changed. A pre-conciliar Catholic who had been brought up on an unrelieved diet of low Masses would have been lost and distressed if he had assisted at a papal Mass celebrated according to the ritual of the *Ordo Romanus Primus*, i.e. the Mass of St Gregory the Great, the Apostle of England. What is sacred in the Mass, any and every Mass, is the saving mystery of Christ which is made present by the celebration. It is this that gives, or should be allowed to give, tonality to the whole celebration however simple. Surely it is not arrogant to say that the "new" Mass has revealed the mystery, as far as mystery can be revealed, that was much obscured by secondary details of the former rite.

Yet even among those who have gladly accepted the new rite, there are misgivings about certain aspects of it and here the approach to what can be forecast for the future will be made through some of these criticisms.

The Ministry of the Word

Strictly speaking the ministry of the word begins with the first reading and extends to and includes the prayers of intercession, but I will take the whole block of material from the beginning of the Mass.

Putting aside the question of the hymn or chant that may begin the Mass, let us consider the entrance rite as it is in the missal. Many have felt that it is both complicated and cumbersome. There are certainly many elements and, what is more important, they do not give a very clear notion of what the community is about as it begins its worship. Yet this is an extremely important moment. If this is not right, it can damage the rest of the celebration. What then is required for the beginning of an act of worship? The first thing that seems to be required is a human contact between the celebrant and the congregation. The remote hieratic attitude of the celebrant of former times and the devout receptive attitude of the "faithful" are no longer sufficient for the inauguration of an act of worship in which all are actively involved and expect to be. Whether there is a need for a set formula (with of course alternatives) or whether if there is one it should *always* have to be used is perhaps debatable. Sometimes the celebrant will be glad to use it and sometimes not. In any case it would seem best that he should state the theme of the Mass or feast and no doubt he himself will find a suitable formula, perhaps drawn from a text of the day. There is a hint of this in a formula composed in Rome for the Mass of 1 January of 1977. The greeting runs: "May God our Father grant that you may live in his grace and in the joy of the Holy Spirit and may the peace of Christ be with you always".[2] This in turn echoes the introit (I think thoughts of peace, says the Lord, and not of affliction). The use of the introit sentence (where appropriate and sometimes it is not) in the greeting restores it to its original purpose of setting the keynote of the Mass. But the introit sentences, especially for the Sundays of the Year, need further examination. Many seem to have been preserved for the sake of the plainsong that went with them.

Then there is the question of the penitential act. As is well known, but apparently not well enough known, this may be varied within the limits of the *pattern* set down. Any one of three formulas may be used, and when the third and best is used the phrases used to arouse people to repentance may vary from week to week. They may be drawn from the gospel of the day or from other texts of the Mass or be adapted to the occasion. Here is a good example of freedom within a given pattern and it is a pity that more use is not made of it. Time should be allowed for it, pauses for silence observed and the whole act conducted with due seriousness. Whether this act should be extended, at least on occasion, and made a formal act of penance is a matter to which we refer below. It is to be hoped that it will be.

This suggests another question: is the act of penance in the right place? Two views were debated, one that it would be best at this point to reconcile the worshippers and prepare them to hear the word of God and the other that the word itself would open people's hearts so that they would be better prepared to receive his forgiveness after it. The first view won the day but the question should not in principle be foreclosed. There is a case for placing it at the end of the prayers of the faithful in which it could be included. It could then be combined with the sign of peace which comes *before* the eucharistic action in every liturgy except the Roman and would be in closer accord with *Matthew 5:23-26* ("Leave your offering before the altar, go and be reconciled. . . and *then* present your offering"). It would of course require a re-arrangement of the communion act but that is in any case a little complicated. Psychologically it would seem to be a better moment. People are more tranquil and receptive than they are in the first moments of the Mass and repentance could become a reality to them.

We are left with the *Gloria* and the collect. If the penitential act were postponed there would not be the very sharp contrast between the penitential mood and the one of praise and joy voiced in the *Gloria*. It would become something more like an entrance hymn, for which it is admirably devised, though it would seem advisable to restrict it to the greater feasts, as it once was. It is hardly possible to be leaping with joy every Sunday of the year.

With the ground thus cleared, the collect would appear for what it is, the prayer of the assembled people, and if the pattern suggested above were adopted it could easily be of greater length than it is and so more prayerful for the people.

The Readings

The restoration of the structure of the ministry of the word which, for many, means simply the addition of another reading and a psalm has not been welcomed with any enthusiasm in some quarters. This is understandable since Catholics, unlike their forefathers in the faith, had become a very *unbiblical* people and the Biblical Revival that accompanied the Liturgical Movement in its later phases passed them by. The Bible was respected but few read it. Few seem to have objected to the miscellany of snippets that formed the lectionary of the 1570 missal whose constant repetition they bore with remarkable equanimity. For the preacher who tried to base his discourses on them, they were a prolonged agony. Many, perhaps most, did not try, and preached out of catechisms or those courses dignified with the title "catechetical" which for the most part were dehydrated doctrine and legalistic morals. For these people the impact of the new lectionary has been heavy though it does not seem to have occurred to them that the remedy is to be found in their reading of the Bible!

Apart however from an allergy to the word of God, there are other more respectable difficulties. Some object to the *length* of the ministry of the word especially in relation to the ministry of the eucharist. Presumably this means that there are those who object to the fact that there are *three* readings, perhaps they would be willing to do without the psalm, and there is, perhaps understandably, a notable lack of enthusiasm for sermons. No doubt there are those who would do away with the first two readings altogether. The Old Testament has never really captured the interest of modern Catholics and although exegetes and theologians (rightly) pay great attention to St Paul, he is not the favourite reading of the laity. They entertain the illusion that they can understand the gospels without reference to anything that went before them. In fact they read the gospels with twentieth century minds.

A more discerning criticism is that the passages to be read are not always as well chosen as they might be. Thus, for the second Sunday of the Year C., the first reading , (*Isaiah 62:1-5*) is about the bridal people of God and the gospel is about the marriage feast of Cana, yet the exegetes tell us that *marriage* as such is not the theme of the Johannine passage.[3] This selection seems to have been dictated by the comparatively modern practice of preaching about Christian marriage on this Sunday. Then when we find that the second reading is about *charismata* and is from *1 Corinthians 12*, one wonders what on earth was in the mind of the compilers. Part of the explanation is that *1 Corinthians* begins on this Sunday in Year A, is continued in Year B and the rest is given in Year C starting with chapter 12! This is called *lectio continua!* For that is the semi-official explanation that has been given for the arrangement of the "epistles" in the new lectionary. Clearly this is not good enough and even when the arrangement is clearer, as for the most part it is, experience has shown that if the passages follow one another on successive Sundays, the people cannot remember what has gone before. It is also clear that sometimes these "epistle" readings are too short, as e.g. Sixth Sunday, Year C, when a mere snippet of the great passage *(1 Corinthians 15)* about the resurrection is given. Something of the sort can be said of the course of reading from the Synoptic Gospels which in general is satisfactory. If, say, for purposes of preaching one examines the gospel text as found in the New Testament, one discovers that from time to time small passages are omitted for reasons that are not clear. In view of these and other difficulties, it will not be surprising if the lectionary eventually undergoes considerable revision. The question then is how best it should be tackled.

One factor, to which I have referred above, that must be taken into account is the increasing inability or unwillingness of people to listen. The reason for that, at least in part, is the distracting life that most people are forced to lead. Yet the remedy is not simply to cut down the amount of reading matter. The reason why the present system is unsatisfactory is that instead of concentrating interest, the lack of coherence in the pattern disperses it.[4] Does this mean that we should go for the "theme" Mass which has had a considerable vogue in recent years?

Wisely I think, the revisers resisted pressures for a series of theme Masses for the ordinary Sundays of the year because, as they said, those asking for them seemed to want to impose themes on the scriptures, themes that would be taken either from the theological manual or someone's scheme of catechetics. This is in fact to do violence to the Bible which has its own theology or rather theologies. It is in this area however that I feel some solution could be found. Certain themes can be found in both the Old and the New Testaments that are often related. The bridal theme is one but it is first an ecclesial theme and is better related to *Mark 1:18-20* than to the Cana miracle. What would be necessary is that the three readings should deliver substantially the same message from different points of view and the psalm could then comment on the whole collection of texts and turn their message into prayer. The gospel would have to remain the pivotal passage and the organisation of the other readings would call for considerable knowledge and skill. It might even be declared to be impossible but surely it should be tried. Nor in this would there be anything fundamentally new. If we look at the texts of the Easter Vigil we find that this is in fact the procedure followed. It was to be found also in the old Ember Day Masses and witnesses to the way the Roman church thought fit to use the scriptures in worship. On the basis of a correct understanding of it, the Bible delivers a coherent message, or, if you like, a series of coherent messages which it may not be too bold to say convey what is essential. In practice this means that it would be necessary to forego the use of certain parts of the Bible in public worship and certainly in eucharistic worship. But that is the situation already. A new scheme would mean that the passages used would be better related to each other.

The suggestion has also been made that there should be no fixed course of reading but that the celebrant should choose such reading or readings as he may think appropriate to the occasion. In some places it would seem it has been (unlawfully) done and is, I understand, the practice of the Free

Churches. It is doubtful however whether this would produce better results than those that come from the use of a fixed lectionary, with all its limitation. For one thing the celebrant as well as the people would have to have a deep understanding of the Bible and an extensive knowledge of it in all its parts. With Catholics at any rate this cannot be assumed. There is also the danger that the *same* parts of the Bible would appear again and again. If we are honest, we all have our favourite parts of the Bible and tend to over-use them. The advantage of the lectionary is that it does confront us with passages of the Bible that we might easily neglect. Likewise, the temptation to build the readings round the sermon would be difficult to resist. The result once again would be to deprive the people of the word of God. Practically, there are few of the parish clergy who would regard with equanimity the need to find appropriate passages every week of the year.

The Homily

The homily or sermon is an integral part of the ministry of the word but it presents peculiar difficulties. One of the most constant sources of complaint about our worship is the poor quality of the discourse given on Sundays. This is not the place to go further into the question. All one would say here is that the *function* of preaching needs to rank higher in the priorities of the clergy and the grounds for so doing are to be found in so accessible a place as the documents of the Second Vatican Council.[5] With this a better training for preaching is still required and needs to be continued for some years after ordination.

A more radical criticism is that the sermon-monologue is no longer suitable in an age when almost everything is done by a process of discussion. Perhaps underlying this is a notion that the priest-celebrant plays too authoritarian a role in the present arrangement and that it would be more in accord with certain current notions of the church that he should not be singled out in this fashion. If this is so, it would be difficult to be very happy about it. The priest by the nature of his office has to bear witness to the word of God and to proclaim it in every way that is open to him. His role here *is* a special one and perhaps it would be more clearly seen if we remembered that this role belonged and still belongs in the first place to the bishop precisely because he is the bond of unity in the church, maintaining the unity of faith and communion in love with other local churchs, and who with the pope forms an essential element in the collegial constitution of the whole church. The other clergy whether priests or deacons receive their mandate to preach from him, a mandate that can be withdrawn. Both bishops and clergy, but especially bishops, have a prophetic role in the church, representing Christ as prophet, and anything that detracted from this would be a deviation from the right order of things.

Once then this position is secured, it becomes a question of whether there are other modalities of bearing witness to the faith than that of the monologue sermon. There would not appear to be any serious objection to this. In talking to children at Mass, for instance, by far the most effective way to teach them is to initiate a dialogue with them. In small groups it has been found that a dialogue or discussion kind of sermon is effective though the priest retains his proper role by initiating and guiding the discussion and summing up at the end. But if people or preacher think that this is going to be an easier way out, they are mistaken. On the people's part a great deal more thought and activity will be required of them and the preacher will have to prepare the subject-matter with great care. Otherwise, it will be just a cosy chat that will lead nowhere.

There are of course considerable practical obstacles to the adoption of such a method for general use. First, there is the matter of time. Discussion takes longer than the ordinary sermon and probably a great deal longer than most people are willing to give to it. Secondly, while this method can be effective with small groups because they are more homogeneous than the parish Sunday congregation, it is doubtful whether it could be effective with the larger groups. Some would feel inadequate and would be unable to take part, others would be too shy and there is always the danger of some few dominating the whole discussion. Bad feeling or even chaos could easily be the result. But need the discussion take place at the eucharist? At least in some places efforts are being made to discuss sermon matter before the celebration with groups who are willing to attend for the purpose and there would seem to be nothing to prevent the discussion being continued afterwards in those places where people gather to drink tea or coffee. This, I understand, often happened in the Welsh chapels when the preacher was invited to dinner and his sermon was made the subject of comment and discussion. What is important and valuable in the method is that the preacher will be in living contact with the people to whom he is trying to give the message of the gospel; he will be learning about their reactions and their needs and will himself receive enlightenment, insights into the gospel message that otherwise he would not have. If the preacher has a prophetic role it is not an exclusive one. There are many gifts, *charismata*, in the one body and among them are wisdom and knowledge. These, as Vatican II says, are distributed throughout the body and are not arbitrarily to be quenched.[6] But these gifts are given for the benefit of the whole church and the priest may profit from them as well as others.

The Creed

Included in the ministry of the word are the creed and the so-called "Bidding Prayers" and something needs to be said about them. First, why the Nicene Creed every Sunday? There is a grave danger here of over-familiarity; the words almost inevitably are said with little or no thought. The Apostles' Creed may be used at least for children's Masses but when in 1964 it was proposed that it should be used as an alternative to the Nicene Creed or perhaps replace it, there was an outcry.[7] There were incautious murmurings about ecumenism from people who hitherto had never showed any enthusiasm for it. They seem to have been unaware that the western version of that creed with the addition of the *Filioque* had been a rock of offence to the Orthodox for centuries. It is to be hoped that in the future both creeds will be in general use.

But I note in *Communautes et Liturgies* a different suggestion.[8] The second reading for Sunday V Year C is *1 Corinthians 15:1-11*, the well known passage about the resurrection appearances. The writer suggests that it might be used in place of the creed. Here he has the exegetes with him who are agreed, or seem to be, that it does represent a primitive creed already in existence when Paul wrote. The writer does not suggest however that it should be recited by the whole congregation. The celebrant is to do that and is to conclude it with the words of verse 11: "This is our message, this is our faith" and the people are to reply with a refrain. Perhaps it is a suggestion worth thinking about though it does represent a duplication. Perhaps a creed based on the passage would be better and could be used with advantage in Eastertide. Other passages of the New Testament would lend themselves to the same treatment: e.g. *Colossians 1:15-20* which professes faith in God as Father and creator, in his Son who is his "image", in the church which is his body and in his saving work of reconciliation. If it were objected that these "creeds" omit certain doctrines, it must be pointed out that even the Nicene Creed is gravely deficient: it does not mention the eucharist! It is of course *au fond* a baptismal creed.

The Prayer of the Faithful

As for the General Intercession or Prayers of the Faithful (in England—alone—"Bidding" prayers) the first thing that needs to be done is to understand their form and only then can development be looked for. These prayers are presided over by the celebrant who introduces and concludes them; the texts are *invitations* to prayer voiced by a minister (deacon) or lay-person; they are addressed to God the Father and not to Christ; the people's prayer is the *response*, which may be various ranging from the brief "Lord, have mercy" to something longer. Present practice seems too often to think of these "invitatories" as prayers in themselves and one has even heard them phrased "Dear Jesus...". According to the General Instruction they are to be concerned with (a) the church, (b) human society, (c) the deprived and oppressed, and (d) the needs of the local community (n. 46). These directives give the basic content of the prayers and are meant to direct local communities away from too great a concern for their own needs. In fact, the prayers need to be very flexible, reflecting the theme or themes of the Mass or the needs of the gathered community. In particular, if they are to

remain living elements of the Liturgy, they will need to be
composed for every Mass and linked to the ministry of the
word of which they are a part (G. I. n. 33). The Roman
Missal in its Appendix gives three models for these prayers.
They begin with *"Pro"* and continue with *"ut"*; a second
formula begins with *"ut"* and a third manages to do without
the *"ut"* but always ends with an invitatory phrase. This
form as given in Latin may provide difficulties in English
where the subjunctive is a dying mood but they can be sur-
mounted with a little thought and ingenuity.

Once their literary form has been understood we can begin
to think of development. In the past these prayers have taken
different forms as we can see from the passages given above
from Clement of Rome which was probably an echo of intercessions in the first century eucharist. There are further indications in Tertullian, and Cyprian.. Prosper of Aquitaine,
the "secretary" of Leo the Great in the fifth century, provides
enough evidence to show that the *Orationes sollemnes* that
survive in the Good Friday liturgy were already in existence.
Here, as mentioned above, we have a longer invitatory, a
pause for silence and the collect of the president who sums
up the people's *prayer*. There is no reason why this form
should not be extended to other occasions especially as it has
the advantage of indicating more specially what the people
are to pray for. The present form seems to derive from the
so-called *Deprecatio Gelasii* of the end of the fifth century
and owes something to eastern liturgies where the form is
always litanic. But neither form is exclusive of the other.

Can we look for further development? On the continent of
Europe this seems already to have taken place. In *Communautes et Liturgies*, for instance, models of prayers are given
which however may evidently be used as they stand. One
feature that is important is that their themes are dictated by
the readings of the day. Here is one example:

"Leaving all things, they followed him."
"How can we dare:
to leave the ship,
give up our job, promotion or reputation,
and go out to
the unemployed,
the stranger threatened with eviction,

the prisoner who is despised?"
Resp. "I am not worthy to come near you, Lord,
    Let your word guide my steps and I shall be healed."
"I will be your messenger. Send me."
"How can we dare to leave the safety of our daily life,
the refuge of a peaceful humility,
to risk going away from our familiar place,
to bring up a numerous family,
to accept heavy responsibility?"
Resp. as before.
"I am what I am by the grace of God."
"How can we dare to recognise our faults and wrong-doing,
without seeking excuses because we are in good faith,
or falling back on our 'conversion';
Can we risk a painful break with our past,
face the demands of faithfulness to a community far from attractive, or those made on us by parents, fallen friends, the aged, the
sick?"
Resp. as before.

These are evidently carefully thought out and are valuable
for the suggestions they give but it is doubtful if they could
be used at the ordinary Sunday Mass. Their form is somewhat
complicated and it is difficult to suppose that the clergy or a
parish group could compose anything like these regularly. The
people too would, I think, be disconcerted by the form
which in any case is envisaged as changing from Sunday to
Sunday.

The next two samples infringe the rule I have mentioned
above: they are prayers.

"In communion with the pope, the bishops, Christian communities, the entire church."
Keep us, Lord, from relying on human devices
instead of drawing our power from the Spirit."
Resp. "Give us a new heart, Lord,
    and put in us a new spirit."

There is more to follow, petitions "for those without hope,
the poor, the destitute, the afflicted, the despised. . ." but all
in this form. As for form, the same can be said (in part) of an
English collection, *Bidding Prayers for the Church's Year* by
David Konstant.[9] Is it too rigid to say that these forms are
undesirable or are they witness to the fact that the form
suggested in the Roman Missal is too difficult to manipulate

in modern languages? I doubt whether this is true of French
though it may be of English. Or is it that people are looking
for a more direct kind of prayer in which they can more
easily express their sentiments? If this is the case, then we
can look for a development of the form of these prayers
which may have its virtues but also its dangers. It opens the
door to the worst kind of pietism and could soon become
formless.

Another form in the same series is more promising:

> "Our sufficiency today should not let us forget
> the situation of yesterday nor that of so many human beings:
> Stateless persons (*vagabonds*) in search of a country,
> immigrants in a strange land,
> the ill-used and those reduced to slavery,
> the poor, the wretched, the oppressed."
> Resp. "Let my prayer come before you like incense
> as I raise my hands in offering at evening time."

The method here is obviously to mention certain categories
of people who call for our prayers and then to make a general
petition in this case with a verse from psalm 140. It is to be
presumed that there is a silence between the statement and
the petition—as there ought to be in any form of the prayer.
If so it could be quite impressive and suggests a form that
could very well be developed in the future.[10]

The Ministry of the Eucharist

A good deal has been said about the eucharistic prayer
above. Here we are concerned primarily with other parts of
the rite.

The Preparation of the Gifts

The situation here is a little confused. The General Instruction (49) says: "Then the gifts are brought up to the altar. . .
the priest or deacon receives them at some suitable point and
places them on the altar. *While doing this* the priest says
some prescribed prayers." The whole passage lacks clarity.
While doing what exactly? While putting the gifts on the
altar? If you go to the *text* of the *Missale Romanum,* you will
see that the priest is instructed to say the "blessing" prayers
over the bread and wine respectively *secreto* but if there is no

singing he *may* recite them aloud and the people may reply. What is not sufficiently clear is whether the priest may *omit* these prayers altogether, at least when there is singing. As is well known, they are relics of the priest's *apologiae* dating from the ninth century. In days when even the clergy went to confession rarely enough they expressed their unworthiness to celebrate and asked for the forgiveness of their sins and they inserted them into certain parts of the liturgy and said them when they had nothing else to do. It would seem that the suppression of these prayers at the offertory was too much for some, though this is what the revisers wanted. A compromise was reached. Two new "blessing" prayers were composed and inserted but some of the others, in emasculated form, were re-inserted. All were only to be said *secreto*. However further pressure got the permissive rubric that the two "blessing" prayers might be said aloud.[11] No one however thought to suggest that they might have been retained for a "low" Mass when few people are present and omitted when the offertory chant is sung. It is to be hoped that in the future this arrangement will become permissible and then we shall have an act that is clear and simple: the bread and wine, — with the money collection — will be brought to the altar during the singing of the chant, the appropriate minister will put them on the altar, the chalice will be mixed, the hands washed (if that not very meaningful act is retained) and the whole rite will be summed up either with a fixed text, the *Orate fratres* (to which the people remain attached) or by the Prayer over the Offerings which usually says little more. A more radical solution would be the suppression of both these prayers and then the phrase of the eucharistic prayers (e.g. EP II: "Let your Spirit come upon these gifts. . .") would have its full force. Such an arrangement would also eliminate what is at present a duplication which the Constitution on the Liturgy (34, 50) said should not be admitted. It is odd that one should be looking for a "simplification" within ten years of the revision of the liturgy.

The Breaking of the Bread

An unauthorised "development" that is taking place in some regions is the breaking of the host during the words of institution. The question is whether it is a desirable development or not. It is a practice that witnesses to a desire for authenticity, simply that in liturgy we should do what we say. But the gesture should be carefully considered before it becomes anything like a custom which might eventually be authorised.

It is a practice that has had a considerable vogue since the Reformation as can be seen from the Communion Service of the Book of Common Prayer.[12] In England and France from the thirteenth century there was a suggestion of the rite. Some missals bade the celebrant to "simulate the fraction" (*fingat frangere*) and this may have influenced the sixteenth century custom. Before that it is extremely rare. It is found among the West Syrians, who were given to dramatising the liturgy, and the Copts who during the words of institution broke the bread into three parts, without separating them. At the fraction before communion they were arranged in the form of a cross.[13] There is not much to go on here.

There is of course the New Testament material. There is the constant phrase used in Acts "the breaking of the bread", used of the eucharist, but there is no clear indication *when* the bread was broken. If the scholars are right, the prayer over the bread, the *berakah*, was a short one and the bread will have been broken at the end of it and then distributed.[14] When the "blessing" prayer over the wine was joined to that over the bread, as it was by the time the New Testament accounts were written, the breaking of the bread and its distribution will have taken place at this moment along with the drinking from the cup.

There is another consideration that must be taken into account. If the New Testament accounts give the main facts of the institution of the eucharist, they do not give a photographic record of, say, the precise succession of events at the Last Supper which can only be deduced, and then partially, by scholarly investigations. In other words it is necessary to make a distinction between what Jesus did at the Last Supper and what the church is doing now. Then, he was acting in the historical order. He was instituting the eucharist which he meant should be continued: "Do this in *memory* of me." The church, obedient to the Lord's command, is making the memorial, the *anamnesis* of the Last Supper, and is not *imitating* action for action what Jesus did then. The Mass is *not* a dramatisation of the Last Supper and the notion that it is has led to all sorts of unhappy deviations. It is the sacramental making present of the essence of what happened at the Last Supper and because it is a sacrament of Christ it can convey to us now all that he intended us to receive. The essence of the eucharist is not the multiplicity of actions that went to make up the Last Supper, some of which are unknown to us, but the paschal mystery of his passion, death, resurrection which the Supper anticipated.

Nor, I think, is it without significance that in all the eucharistic prayers of antiquity there is always an *anamnesis* after the words of institution. In this prayer we can see the desire of the church to ponder on the meaning of "making the memorial" and this, expressed in a prayer, delays the fraction. If the epiclesis of the Holy Spirit is as early as the beginning of the third century — we find it in the present text of Hippolytus — this was another prayer that at a quite early date delayed the breaking of the bread. When later still intercessions and/or the memento of the dead were added, there was yet further delay.

In conclusion it must be said that if the bread is to be broken during the words of institution, those who favour the gesture should be consistent with themselves. The narrative says not only that the Lord broke the bread but that he said, "Take and eat." Communion should be given at once. It must remain very doubtful whether the fraction at this place is an authentic development.

The Doxology

Another "unauthorised" practice that seems to be widely used is the recital by the people of the doxology. This too is an undesirable practice for the doxology is part of the presidential prayer and it belongs to him to say it. If all say it together I do not know who is saying *Amen* to whom. It is one more way of reducing that important response to the status of a punctuation mark. No doubt if the interventions I have mentioned above were introduced the desire to say the doxology would disappear.

The Rite of Communion

Very clearly in the new rite the Lord's prayer begins the act of communion. In a number of eastern liturgies it follows the fraction that takes place at the end of the eucharistic prayer and this seems to be the more logical place. It owes its present place in the Roman rite to the desire, it would seem, of Pope Gregory the Great to say this prayer over the consecrated elements at the altar and before he went to his throne where previously the whole of the communion action had taken place. Although it would involve some re-arrangement of the communion act, it would seem desirable in the interests of clarity and simplicity, asked for by the Constitution on the Liturgy (34), that the fraction should take place immediately after the eucharistic prayer and with an appropriate formula. Then the Lord's prayer with the sign of peace and the rest would follow making a clear act wholly concerned with the giving of communion.

The importance of the act of communion does not yet seem to have penetrated Catholic consciousness or at least clerical consciousness. For the people it is the supreme moment when, according to all the documents, they make their deepest participation in the eucharist. Yet holy communion is still given in an almost clinical way, small white wafers are put into people's mouths and the whole act is carried out as quickly as possible, sometimes more quickly than is reverent. Yet the remedy is available. First the permission to give communion in both kinds is usually readily available but this practice still seems to be rare in parish churches. One reason for this no doubt is the difficulty for a single minister to give communion in both kinds to a large congregation. The time taken is considerable and if the people have to return to the altar for the chalice, as they will, it is hardly elegant. In some places the people receive the host and drink from the chalice that is set on a table nearby—not a practice to be recommended. The chalice should be administered. This practice turns everyone in the church into a minister of holy communion! Secondly, the remedy is the institution of lay-ministers who will assist the celebrant. There is nothing new in this of course; for some years it has been common practice in many dioceses and in many different parts of the world. Where there is an insufficiency of priests it has become a necessity and all the signs are that Great Britain will before long experience a similar need. It would seem the plainest common sense to increase the number of lay-ministers everywhere and not wait until the deluge (or should it be famine?) is upon us. The advantages of so doing are considerable. The laity will be brought closer to the clergy since they will be sharing both liturgically and pastorally in some of their most important work. For such ministers not only share with the priest the administration of communion in the Mass, they are able to give communion to the sick and housebound and to do it far more frequently than is normally possible for the clergy.[15] In this way they will also share in the pastoral care of the sick as the church desires and indeed urges in the Order for the Pastoral Care of the Sick (33).

As experience has shown, there will be some resistance to the institution of such ministers. There are those who argue that the administration of communion is *specifically* a priestly act, i.e. one that only an ordained minister can perform. There is no ground for this. In the early church the laity took home the consecrated elements (the bread most probably intincted with the consecrated wine) and communicated themselves during the week. On other occasions they have been instructed to consume consecrated hosts to save them from profanation or fire. There are others who think that the lay-person is not "holy" enough and that it is not "reverent" for one such to give holy communion. Here we touch on something that comes close to taboo. However, all these things need explaining and the best people to do this are the bishops. If a lead is given, if the lay-ministers are publicly instituted by the bishop or his delegate, much of the opposition melts away.

Another reason for the failure to give communion in both kinds is mental inertia, a failure to think about the liturgy and its meaning. For nearly nine hundred years Catholics of the West have been used to communion in one kind alone. It

is a practice that has proved itself and there is theological
justification for it in the theory of concomitance. Why
should anyone want to change? As usual, there is a hiatus
between theology and liturgy. Liturgy is concerned with
doing and the doing is rooted in what Christ did at the Last
Supper. Whatever hackles are (still?) raised by saying that the
Mass is a "meal", there is no denying that it is one and that
that is how it all began. But at a meal there is both eating and
drinking and the full significance (the symbolism) of the
eucharist is impoverished if communion in one kind is the
unvarying practice. In the last analysis it is a question of
authenticity. Is it tolerable to say one thing, "Take and eat,
Take and drink" and then do another? As people overcome
their inhibitions I feel sure that in the years to come communion in both kinds with the help of lay-ministers will
become regular practice.

Then there is the practice of giving communion regularly
from the tabernacle. Church authority, from Benedict XIV in
the eighteenth century to Vatican II in the twentieth, has
deprecated it and urged that people should be communicated
from bread consecrated at the Mass they attend. If one con-
siders the pattern of the eucharist for a moment, the failure
to consecrate *for* communion is a striking anomaly.[16] At the
Last Supper Christ gave his body (gave it up to death) and his
blood (gave his life) that his followers might eat and drink
and so receive his life into themselves. The eucharist is a
single action even if there are different "movements" within
it but all go to make up one whole. The unity of the action is
broken when communion is not given from the bread and
wine consecrated in the one action.

There is another aspect of the matter, one that concerns
the radical symbolism of the eucharist. It is the one bread,
said St Paul, that makes us one body in Christ. Yet at the
eucharist today there are many "breads" and when communion is given from the chalice usually many cups. Practical
difficulties about doing anything else are urged but since
union, the union of Christians with Christ *and* with one
another ("com-union") is the principal symbol of the eucharist we ought at least to try to do the right thing whenever it is
possible. For instance, it is always possible to break up the

large host and communicate at least some of the assembly
from it and it is usually possible to communicate them from
the one cup, *provided* it is not one of those tulip-like vessels
that date from the eighteenth century. Larger chalices are
now available and, for those who will look for them, "hosts"
that *look* more like bread and that can often be made in
different sizes. If we are to look for an even greater simplicity,
for situations where complicated apparatus for the Mass
would be out of place, we should have to contemplate the
use of ordinary bread, as many have already suggested. These
and many other matters are concerned with the authenticity
of symbols which must be as closely related to the realities
which is their point of departure, an authenticity which is
necessary if they are to convey fully the reality for which
they have been chosen, in this case, chosen by Christ himself.

These may all seem to be minor matters of ritual, without
importance in a world that is full of strife, suffering and difficulties of all kinds. That is true and a concern for ritual
matters without a concern for the world is unhealthy. But
what one hopes is that a liturgy that is simple and meaningful
over its whole range will do something to reveal the central
mystery that is the redeeming Christ whose mission for the
salvation of the world is continued in the church, by its proclamation of his word and the celebration of his sacraments.
Nor can the eucharist be seen in abstraction from the community, the world and the people of the world who celebrate
it or whom we hope to draw into its celebration. The total
sign of the eucharist, as the Constitution on the Liturgy
makes clear, is the worshipping community. It is they who
manifest in all its breadth and depth the redeeming work of
Christ as it is made present in the eucharist. The changing
nature of the community will affect the celebration of the
eucharist and it is to this aspect of that matter that we now
turn.

7 The Community

If the discussion or dialogue sermon, as adumbrated above, were ever to become a normal method of preaching it is clear that the community engaged in it would have to be smaller than is customary in our churches on Sundays today. But this suggests lines of thought that are not so much concerned with liturgy in the narrower sense as with the people with whom it is to be celebrated and the milieu in which it is to be celebrated. For one thing, the generalised sermon which seeks to say something to the L.C.M. or very optimistically the H.C.F. of a miscellaneous community whose IQ might range from the near-subnormal to the brilliant, has long been questioned as an adequate means of conveying the Christian gospel. *If* the general level of the Sunday discourse is good, there is a case for saying that its effect is cumulative rather than immediate. But it is not only a matter of sermons. For some time now there have been complaints that the usual parish assembly is impersonal. There is, people say, a lack of human contact and perhaps they are too shy to say that there is a lack of contact with the Divine. A celebration for a large crowd is certainly very difficult to organise if it is to "hook" those present or at least some of them. There are other factors too. In most parts of the world there is a decreasing number of priests to serve the people. Even in England where the parishioner-priest ratio is still good, it looks as if that on average a priest in urban parishes is in charge of about 2,000 people. If anything like personal relations are to be maintained with the priest this is an impossible number and real relationships between the people highly improbable. There is at the moment little reason to suppose that the situation will improve and several to suggest that it will get worse. The question then has to be asked: will the parish *as we know it* exist in fifty years time?

The problems seem to be both quantitative and qualitative. With the increasing shortage of clergy it seems improbable that dioceses will be able to maintain the number of parishes that now exist, that is parishes with however small a staff (one or two full-time priests) and a given number of people. The combining of parishes is no real solution. It merely means that the same number of priests (or perhaps fewer) will have to look after more people scattered over a wider area. Qualitatively the community will suffer because anything like a personal relationship between priest and people will be more difficult to maintain and the people themselves, belonging to different milieux, will have less sense of cohesion than they have now.

In the thinking about this matter, two tendencies can be noted. One looks towards the formation of much smaller groups, whether they be called parishes or not, consisting of about thirty people who because they know each other as persons would be a true community. These would gather together week by week for "worship, charity, witness and apostolate" under the guidance of a priest.[1] It is conceived that they would belong to a larger grouping that for convenience we can call the parish and would be integral parts of it. There is much to be said for such an arrangement. The smaller group facilitates a sense of community among its members and as such can contribute to the building of community in the larger grouping. When, as is desirable, the sub-groups of the parish met together, there would be a range of horizontal relationships between the members of the groups. Their spirit of "relatedness" would stimulate a like spirit in others who may not have had the same opportunities. Nor would the "parish" become superfluous. Far from it. A group as small as thirty would have a number of limitations, e.g. in the ability to teach its children, perhaps in music, and almost certainly in financial resources, these latter envisaged as being needed not so much for the group itself as for the charitable work it would wish to do for others.

The other tendency, not opposed to the former, is to look for larger groupings on the scale of a deanery or something of the kind. There would be a sharing of human and spiritual

resources that few parishes in fact possess. These would
include people with specialist training such as catechists and
youth workers. As to the first, there are not only large numbers of children outside Catholic schools but there is also the
need, as is widely agreed nowadays, to promote the adult
education of Christians.[2] The provision made by the church
is meagre in the extreme and yet everyone seems deeply concerned about the loss of the younger element of the Catholic
community. But both catechists and youth-workers need to
have status and to be paid. This raises the question of finance.
A larger grouping should be able to find the money to
finance such work and there is no doubt that it would be well
spent. The effectiveness of the secondary school in conveying
a living faith to its students is more and more being called
into question and there is a case, based on experience, for
saying that Christian education given outside the school context is more effective. Adequately paid and established jobs
would, among other things, ensure a certain continuity of
work in these fields which is usually impossible to secure
with voluntary labour. These and other tasks would require
different thinking on the matter of finance and different
methods of handling it. It would seem to follow that some
sort of administrator would be needed for this larger grouping and he (or she) would best be a lay-person who would of
course need paying also. A group of parishes could afford to
do so and the clergy would be released from a number of
material chores and would be more free to do the pastoral
work for which they were ordained.

The pastoral work of the region would of course have to
be planned. Men with a talent for certain kind of work
should be allowed to do it across the whole region, but all
would need to meet at regular intervals to see that all the
work planned is being carried out and to discover whether
there are needs that are not being met. This would ensure
that the clergy think and work together in a way that has not
been known in the past. A sense of community, based on
common concerns, would grow among the clergy themselves.
This would be a great strength and incidentally do something
to eliminate the sort of clerical idiosyncracy that is counter-
productive of sound pastoral practice. It would mean of

course that the parish would lose something of its independence but that is a quality that on the whole has been overvalued. It seems rather absurd that people holding the same faith and belonging to the same church which by definition is "catholic" should be confined to separate non-communicating compartments. That is how it once was, at least in theory, but if it ever worked, it does not do so now.

In fact, the two tendencies converge. What is sought is the creation of communities where people can know each other, share common problems and be human in a world that is increasingly inhuman. But a relationship with a large community is also seen to be necessary. The smaller community cannot hope to meet all its needs and association with a wider community would do much to eliminate the danger of the formation of inward-looking elites. Ideally—and the whole suggestion may seem hopelessly idealistic to some—the diocese will be the wider community and a realistic union with it would bring the smaller communities fully within the main stream of church life. As is well known, dioceses are going to be divided and multiplied though the plans before the church in this country at the moment still seem to suggest that new dioceses will be too big for the development of the community spirit. That there are difficulties, most of an administrative and financial kind, goes without saying but it is at this point that the church authorities—and indeed those not in authority—need to examine their priorities. *Salus populi suprema lex*, as Pope John liked to quote. If certain new patterns and the arrangements that flow from them can be seen to assist in the salvation of the people, then they should be adopted whatever the difficulties.

The Servants of the Community

The multiplication of smaller groups would obviously require more priests and they are sadly in short supply. On present forecasts the situation is not going to get better and it would seem to be wise to think about the future now. Is there any way whereby a sufficiency of priests could be obtained? Anything like an adequate answer is difficult to come by because we really do not know why recruitment is so meagre. Everyone has his or her notion of the cause but even if all the notions were put together they would not provide the necessary information since we are all speculating out of a limited experience. One of the difficulties however about which there is a measure of agreement is that a life-long commitment to priesthood and celibacy, such as is required at the moment, is daunting to a generation and indeed a whole society that does not seem to have developed beyond adolescence. Vocation directors have for some time been looking for vocations among young men (rather than boys) but this is not proving very fruitful. Young men of eighteen or nineteen have usually been "going steady" for two or three years with a girl. In the promiscuous society in which we live this is often seen as a protection and is to be respected as such. But it does mean that these young men are not candidates for ordination! It is altogether another question whether celibacy as a condition for ordination to the priesthood would lead to an increase of candidates and since the question at the moment is no more than academic there is no point in discussing it here.

The key word however seems to be "maturity" and this prompts one to look in another direction. One suggestion that has been discussed with reasonable calm is the ordination of married men of mature age.[3] Neither laity nor clergy, with whom at one time or another I have discussed the matter, have shown serious opposition to it though whether there would be opposition if married men were in fact ordained is another matter. People, especially perhaps English people, will let a discussion roll for quite a long time in the belief that of course nothing will be done about the subject under discussion.

However as the situation worsens—and some parishes are already finding it difficult to maintain the current Mass schedule—people may be willing to contemplate the possibility of "part-time" priests. As the possibility or even the likelihood of having no resident priest become more imminent, as people reflect that with ever rising petrol prices they will have to travel some distance to Mass, perhaps they will regard the ordination of married men with equanimity, even with favour. As the society in which they live becomes ever more impersonal—there seems little hope of reversing the trend—they will welcome the existence of a small Christian

community where they can experience human relationships
and be drawn on to a deeper relationship with God. In the
last resort it would be for the bishops to put the matter fairly
and squarely before the people in good time and with reasons
given. One reason why it should be discussed in a realistic
way now is that we still have time to do so, though not as
much as some seem to think. We have time to plan and even
perhaps to experiment. What is certainly to court disaster is
to make decisions under pressure of events and when there is
insufficient time to plan.

There is of course the great obstacle of the present legislation of the church on celibacy and the priesthood and it is
impossible to forecast at present whether the supreme
authority of the church will see it as expedient to make a
change. Here one would have thought *salus populi suprema
lex* was eminently applicable. One thing Catholic people want
before anything else is the eucharist. One theological truth
that is accepted by all is that the eucharist makes community
and for this priests are necessary. Surely it is logical to *act* on
a principle if we hold it to be true: *lex credendi, lex orandi.*
The nexus between holy orders and celibacy has in any case
been breached with the revival of the permanent deacon who
may be married. The permanent deacon can do useful and
important work in and for the church but one thing he
cannot do is celebrate the eucharist.

From what has been already said it is clear that the
function of such a priest would be primarily that of minister
of the eucharist. *As one of the community* and now endowed
with the order of priesthood he would preside over and celebrate the eucharist which would be seen more fully to be the
action of the whole community. But he would also be the
minister of baptism and it is clear that the celebration of that
sacrament within the eucharist and in the midst of an assembly that has something of a family dimension would be particularly appropriate. But it would be necessary to have a common policy about baptism within the whole parish and to
secure uniformity of practice the parish priest would have to
be informed both before and after the event. The baptism
would be recorded in the parish register and the parish would
remain the normal place of resort for certificates or verifica-

tions of baptism.

For the sacrament of marriage there are a number of canonical requirements that have to be met and the parish priest is the proper person to handle these matters. But once the preliminary interview or interviews are over there is much to be said for the instruction of the prospective bride and bridegroom in the nature and duties of marriage by a married priest with, it is to be hoped, the assistance of his wife. They will be able to speak out of the experience of their own marriage and the theology of the sacrament will be conveyed in the concrete terms of Christian living. The wedding will of course take place in a parish church and the priest who has instructed the couple will if possible take part.

He will of course be the normal minister of the sacraments of those of the community who are ill, anointing, holy communion and viaticum, though emergencies would have to be handled by the permanent staff of the parish. These however seem to occur less and less nowadays. He will assist the dying and take part in the funeral service of the dead. This, it would seem, will most appropriately take place in the parish church where many of the whole community can be gathered. Finally, it would be highly desirable that he should be the leader in prayer of his community. Worship does not consist only of sacraments. There will be times when he can gather the little community together, perhaps when a family is undergoing stress of one kind or another, when there are special needs of the church and the world to pray for. His principal though not exclusive instrument for this will be the Prayer of the Church which is now so flexible in its structure as to make its use possible and effective in a wide variety of circumstances.

But his function would not be restricted to the celebration of the liturgy. Outside the liturgy he will be engaged in the formation of the community he is to serve. It will be his task to gather together those who are to make up the group by making contacts with Catholics and any others who are willing to listen to him. He will gather them together for discussions (out of which the sermon can be shaped) about the problems of the community and the district. Through his relationship with his fellow-clergy in the parish or region and with the bishop of the diocese he will bring to the local group the concerns and needs of the wider church. In such discussions the parish priest should be asked to take part from time to time to maintain the cohesion of the group within the parish. The opinions and concerns of the group will help the parish priest also for he will be in direct contact with people and will learn in what direction their minds are moving. It is clear that a genuine collaboration between the "official" clergy and the "part-time" priest would have to take place if the system were to work successfully. But again, there is nothing new in this. Where there are several priests in a parish they are supposed to work together and if they do not, the effectiveness of their work is impaired.[4] No doubt gifts of tolerance, understanding and good humour are required if pastoral work is to be done on these terms. But granted this—and why should it not be granted?—it is possible to forecast that the pastoral and missionary work of the church will be more effective when done in this simple and unassuming way. On these terms there would be a true presence of a church that *cares* and this seems to be the only sort of church that is going to draw people to itself or, rather, to Christ.

The ordination of mature married men might of course cause difficulties. It would be a new departure for the Catholic church of the Roman rite and not everyone would take to it kindly. Lay-people might well object on the score that they are being put off with a second best. There is the possibility of tensions, disagreements and even jealousies between the "official" clergy and the "part-time" clergy, especially if the latter seemed to be more successful in their ministry. These are human problems which as Christians we are supposed to be able to solve and it would be a sorry comment on the quality of the Christian life in the church that a development, which any way may be forced on us, should be hindered because of dangers like these. Even in the present system where parish priests and their assistants, sometimes forty years younger than their rectors, have to work together, and in Great Britain live in the same house, not all is always sweetness and light. There is perhaps a more serious danger, namely that there would come into being a two-tier system of clergy. The "professionals" who would have a more pro-

longed academic training and the others who would not. The
solution to that problem would be a renewed and deeper
appreciation of *mission*. It would have to be seen that *both*
were engaged in the same work, that *both* had been called by
God and the community, even if in different ways and at
different times of a man's life, to preach the gospel and celebrate the sacraments. *Both* are at the service of the people
and *both* will reach out to people in different ways. In fact,
looking over the history of the church, the parish clergy have
not been conspicuous for their missionary zeal. For a variety
of reasons they have usually tended to look after what exists,
the "flock" committed to their charge. The penetration of a
district by small groups under the guidance of a eucharistic
minister would be *more* effective in reaching people than the
present system.

There are two further questions. The first is the support of
the "part-time" priest. What is envisaged here is that the
priest would already have an occupation and that he would
not be dependent on the offerings of the people for his living.
When he came to retire, if he had insufficient to live on, the
group would supplement his income. When the Catholic
people are provided with Mass and a priest they have never
been found wanting in supporting him. If this arrangement
prove difficult or impossible, it would seem reasonable to ask
the larger community to help and in view of the fact that
assistants (curates) have already become rare, money that
would go to the upkeep of a curate could be diverted to the
support of the "part-time" priest.

Then there is the question of his preparation for the ministry. If a man is working whether in office or factory or
wherever he may work, it would seem the greatest of pities to
take him out of his milieu for any length of time. He could
receive whatever instruction he needed either in evening
classes or by correspondence courses or by both. From time
to time he would attend a closed conference where the
instruction could be intensified and, more important still, he
could be taught about liturgy, prayer and the main principles
of the spiritual life. The methods of the Open University
could be adapted for the training of more mature vocations.
Likewise for such a man the period of service as a deacon

which involves preaching, the celebration of certain sacraments and liturgical acts, and getting to know people by visiting and in other ways, would be of crucial importance. At the end of it the bishop and his advisers would know if the man was suitable for ordination to the priesthood.

As to what he should be taught, there would seem to be no need even to attempt to turn him into a professional theologian. The seminary system in any case, for all its six years study, has not been very successful in this respect. What a man needs is a solid knowledge of the Bible from which he has to preach every Sunday and this teaching will not be simply an academic study. It should go hand in hand with an ability to *use* the Bible in homilies and other methods of teaching. In a word, a good course in catechetics, with constant reference to practice, would seem to be what is required. This will ensure that he has a grasp of the doctrines of the faith and at the same time an ability to communicate. Whether or not he should be commissioned to hear confessions and so have some initiation in moral theology is a matter that might be discussed. But whatever is to be the content of the course—and no doubt experience would show in greater detail what this should be—it would need to be oriented to what the man is going to do, the circumstances in which he is going to do it, and not towards some sort of safety-net to preserve him from preaching heresy. It is surely one of the odder features of our present system that men can preach for years without any kind of supervision whatever.

Whatever instruction such a man should receive, his human qualities would be of the highest importance: understanding of people, an approachable manner, a willingness to work with others, whether lay or clerical, an ability to form community. These will be the means through which he will convey the message of the gospel. If this should seem to be setting the ideal too high, it can be said that for centuries the ideal of the parish clergy has been set very high and that an ideal is something to be striven for. Just as marriages do not happen but have to be made, so has the life of the priest, any priest.

Finally, there is the question of "maturity". In the case of married men what will be looked for is a marriage that has proved itself over the years, one where there is a deep union between husband and wife, who have shown that they can work together in the bringing up of their family. For the wife too will need to have a "vocation", a desire to work for the church and a willingness to help her husband in the new tasks that will be his by virtue of his ordination. As for age, it is to be expected that the children will have grown up and are independent of continual parental care. An ability to undertake some further education would also be required. Men of this sort are already to be found in our parishes and it is improbable that there would be any shortage of suitable candidates.

Given then the existence of such communities it is difficult to believe that any local need would go unnoticed and the smaller group, with perhaps the help of the large community, would bend its effort to meet the need.

In these circumstances it is not difficult to predict that the liturgy of such a community would be a simpler, less formal kind of celebration than that which takes place in most parish churches. Experience shows too that such liturgies offer a deeper and richer experience of the mysteries they celebrate. The members of the community would be like those of the communities of the Acts of the Apostles, one in mind and heart. If there were differences among them it would be seen that reconciliation is not merely desirable but an absolute necessity. Otherwise the community would fall apart. The relevance of the needs of the community to the eucharist, whether it be those of the Christian community itself or those of the community outside it, would be immediately apparent. Any indifference to the needs of others, of whatever kind, would be seen at once to be an anomaly to people who are seeking union with Christ and with each other and the very meaning of whose worship is to offer themselves and their lives to God through Christ. The unhappy gap between life and worship would be closed. Yet the liturgy of such a group need not be dull. The atmosphere of warmth that comes from the gathering together of a small group is a guarantee that the liturgy itself will reflect that warmth. Singing, too, in such groups is quite possible, provided people get over the urge to imitate an old-fashioned high Mass.

Whatever else may be said of the current liturgy, this at least is true, that it is adaptable to a considerable variety of circumstances. The old, rigid division between low Mass (dull) and high Mass (exciting?) has gone. In the new Mass-liturgy there are many texts, such as the phrases of the penitential act, the acclamation after the consecration, the Lord's prayer and its embolism, that lend themselves to simple settings that are within the compass of a small community. The responsorial psalm, which by its nature demands to be sung, may present greater difficulties though even these can be overcome. By the present rules the psalm *need not* be different every Sunday: e.g. one psalm may be used for the first four Sundays of Lent and the first part of Advent. If the psalm is chosen (from the lectionary) with care it will be appropriate to the readings of these periods. Again, if there is but one singer of competence he or she can sustain the verses and lead the rest of the group in singing the responses or indeed anything else that needs singing. The method has been used in France for a long time. Again, we have learned that single instruments, guitar, recorder, violin and, especially for children, the piano are suitable to accompany all sorts of singing that can be expected in a small group. We have learnt that plummy Victorian organs are not necessary (if they ever were) and the famous harmonium, so much beloved of the French clergy in the nineteenth century, seems to have become almost extinct. What is quite certain is that it is the most difficult instrument in the world for the human voice to cope with.

What we may envisage then is a series of small communities, scattered over a certain area, whether urban or rural, that will manifest in their worship the love of God that makes them one and will carry it to others so that it will be expressed in service, in action, and then God's love will be truly present among people. It is difficult to believe that this union of worship and service would not draw people to Christ. The church will appear for what it is, not buildings great or small, rich or poor, but *people*, the humble people of God who own no more than their neighbours, who live like their neighbours, and yet are ready to give of what they have to those in need.

The Permanent Diaconate

In the foregoing chapter little has been said about the permanent diaconate now in use in many parts of the church. The reason for this is that though the permanent deacon can perform a very important role in the pastoral work of the church, he is by definition an assistant of the priest (as well as being the servant, *diaconos*, of the people) and if the number of priests is decreasing, as it is, his usefulness is somewhat limited. As I have said above, what the people want above all is a eucharistic minister. However, from a document drawn up by Archbishop Worlock (Liverpool) and presented for study to the Bishops' Conference it is possible to see how to go about the business of selecting men of mature years for the *priesthood*.

1. The document urges that the testimony of the candidate's colleagues, apostolic or interest group, as well as the local parish should be sought. Given this, the parish priest is to have a decisive say in the selection.

2. The second conclusion we can draw from the document is that the man should have a strong pastoral sense. The "sacristy" type is to be avoided. It is envisaged that he should work with a local community, that he should be the "animator of an outlying part of the parish" or of some group or groups engaged on special work.

3. He is to be required to answer a questionnaire of nine items giving his view of the diaconate, his sense of vocation to the Order and other background information about his life. If married, his wife is to be brought into full consultation and her willingness to support him in his office is regarded as a necessity.

4. Two years of formal study is asked for, though normally, it would seem, residence in a house of study will not be required. The subjects cover holy scripture, an initiation into theology, with special attention to sacramental theology, moral theology in so far as it is relevant to his work, preaching, catechetics for adults and children and spiritual formation. If he is to do some special work (the deprived, the handicapped etc.) he is to be prepared for it.

Here then is a thoroughly worked out scheme for the train-

ing of deacons and most of it would be applicable and appropriate as a preparation of priests of mature age. However, the
role of the parish priest in the process of selection seems to
be rather over-emphasised and that of the local community a
little under-emphasised. This may indicate that consultation
procedures in parishes still leave something to be desired.
Although "the ability range is likely to be as academically
varied as that for the priesthood", the study requirement
seems to be rather high. However, a man is not to be taken
out of his milieu—which is a good thing. One very positive
observation speaks of "building up communities" and this, as
I have said above, will be a crucial role of the eucharistic
minister. It is also stated that he must be acceptable to the
community he is called to serve. That too is a most important
point; without acceptance it is difficult to imagine either
priest or deacon being able to work effectively. But how is
the local community to indicate its acceptance?

There is much else in the document worthy of attention
and if some such scheme gets under way, it will be a very
useful forerunner of a similar scheme for priests. It should
however be remembered that this document is more in the
nature of a working paper than a final scheme. The bishops
have yet to consider it and bring it into force.[5]

8 The Presentation of the Liturgy

The remarks made above on the audio-visual liturgy may have seemed flippant but there are serious issues here. If worship is directed to God it is the worshipping community that has to be raised up to him and that community is made up of ordinary human beings. The church in worship has to accept them as they are and at least start from where they are though that does not mean that it must leave them where they are. Yet everyone is aware that it is difficult to lead people from where they are to something better. The gap between culture, music, the visual arts, literature and the rest, and what might be called popular culture, seems to be widening though both witness to certain fundamental human needs that have been denied in a civilisation that put great emphasis on the mind, on literarcy and non-audio-visual values. Poetry that, as far as we can see, began as song or at least as declamation came to be a highly complicated exercise which was first written down and then recited, if it was recited at all. Blind Homer can hardly have *written* the Iliad. Rather like the Old Testament prophets he will have declaimed his saga which had to be good enough to hold the attention of his audience. The lyric was, according to the Oxford Concise Dictionary "meant to be sung" to the accompaniment of a lyre. The chorus of the early Greek plays was a dance as was the later carol. Action, words, song were the constituent parts of "literature". For more than two thousand years western culture has been so literary that failure to appreciate its products was to earn the opprobrium of being "uncultured". The arrogance underlying this assumption has not, I think, always been discerned and association with those who make things, with painters, sculptors, workers in metal or in other media shows that there is a culture of the senses usually combined with insights into the nature of things. Artists, whether they have a religious faith or not, often show themselves more open to religious considerations than those who have cultivated the purely rational side of human nature. Crudely perhaps, those who have been culturally *déclassés* are having their revenge and what millions are experiencing through media that have become debased, or were always so, has an important message for the church.

Light

Christian liturgy has always made use of a variety of media to convey the message of the gospel, words, music, gesture, ceremonial, lights, and colour. The manner of using them became stereotyped so that people hardly noticed what was before them, until at least some of it was taken away. Hence the dismay of some who were attached to the "old" Mass as a cultural art-form. Up to a point their dismay is understandable. The old Mass as an art-form could be very beautiful, as for example a well conducted high Mass (though so often it was not), but it was the art-form of an earlier age. Most people cannot live in the past and we know that it is dangerous to live *on* it. That way lies bankruptcy. The point of these observations is that since the Christian liturgy has never been purely a mental thing, the task that lies before us is to revalue the media that have been used and to explore new possibilities that lie open to us. Already there have been changes that have gone unobserved. The "dim religious light" of the Gothic and neo-Gothic church, which was all very well when people *watched* a service, the gloom and distance enhancing the view, is a thing of the past. Even ancient Gothic churches are now for the most part lit up in a way that enhances the building, the locale of worship, and adds a note of life and warmth to the celebrations that take place there. In modern churches it has of course been possible to do more, though oddly enough the possibilities of exploiting light and space have not always been realised. Floods of light on the sanctuary or floods of light on the auditorium flatten surfaces, are tiresome because they disperse interest and untimately become boring. The lighting of a church, and of everything within it, needs to be carefully planned according to the needs of the liturgy. The focus of the eucharistic liturgy changes during the course of its celebration. There is the entrance procession when the light of the sanctuary could be dimmed. There is the introduction done by the president when some emphasis in light on the place where he stands is in order. The centre of interest then passes to the ministry of the word and if a microphone has been accepted as necessary, why should not some light be also regarded as necessary to enhance the role of the word of God in the assembly? For the eucharistic action proper light needs to be concentrated on the altar where too there will be a microphone. Sight and sound go together.

Colour

As with light, so with colour. It needs to be used imaginatively and too many modern churches are stark and puritanical in appearance. Decorators of secular buildings have often been far more successful; they have varied the colours of different walls and used different textures in the same space to give life to it. Though more thought should be given to such devices in decoration of churches, it is not just a matter of colouring surfaces. They can pall after a time and an austere background is a splendid foil for an object whether it be a crucifix, a tapestry or a statue. If these are good, good to look at for themselves, their background will enhance their qualities. But what is needed more than anything else is changeable and movable objects that will make the point of a particular occasion, feast or season. We already have the Crib at Christmas and in some places the Easter Garden for the resurrection though too often it suggests dead vegetation rather than the triumph of Life. But more than this is required. A tapestry behind the altar or a pallium covering it can convey the message of the feast. For saints' days a banner with a figure of the saint could be set up in the most convenient place, perhaps surrounded by candles and flowers. And since statues can be made in a variety of materials nowadays, some of which are not heavy, there is no reason why they should not be put in place for the day and taken away afterwards. What we see all the time we hardly notice. In fact many of these devices are being used already. Their use only needs to become more common.

Movement

When we come to movement we enter a sphere that to many seems dangerous for it spells the word "dance". But before closing our minds to its possible use in liturgy let us reflect that one of the more important features of the Christian liturgy is its use of movement. Processions, the organised movement of a body of people usually to the accompaniment of song and music, from one sacred place to another, have been a constant element in Christian worship that were at one time regarded as of great importance. The Rogation processions on St Mark's day and the three days before the Ascension took worship out into the fields, into the life of millions of ordinary men and women who earned their living from the cultivation of the land. That the effects of such processions (they were apotropaic, warding off evil influences, including harmful insects) were often in the minds of the people a kind of magic is neither here nor there for the moment. Here was mobile worship that, in some places, such as Echternacht, took on the form of a solemn dance. The procession of Palm Sunday, now intended to be a true procession from one place to another, the processions of our Lady in May and that of *Corpus Christi* after Trinity Sunday are still with us and if they are to be worthy of their purpose need organisation and choreography. Inside the church too there has always been movement, sometimes of a quite elaborate kind, but it was confined to the clergy and their trained helpers, the altar servers. It has often been remarked that the old High Mass was based on a certain choreography even if the performers were unaware of it.

In recent years there has been a limited revival of the liturgical dance, the most famous of which is probably the Drama of the Mass that took place in the Metropolitan Cathedral at Liverpool after the consecration of the church. A description of it indicates certain important truths: "The project simply took the mass as its theme. No real mass was celebrated; there was no priest; and the central altar remained bare and unused. But what was created was a *visual express-*

ion of the prayers of the mass. The director and choreographer, Bill Harpe, used choreography as an independent and autonomous 'voice'. *Images* of worship, suffering, pain, glory, hope and so on were expressed in simple, modern dances. *At the same time* the choir and orchestra performed the music of a 17th century mass setting by the Italian, Francesco Cavalli, a pupil of Monteverdi. *The mass therefore had two 'voices'*—the music and the choreography—*and they came together as marriage* partners."[1] Music, light and movement were brought together to convey the meaning of the mass, but the audience remained passive, hearers and viewers. Another experience described by the same writer involved the whole assembly: a "pop" version of familiar carols "proved irresistible and the congregation simply started to dance. . . There was no finesse about the dancing, but it was none the less a genuine physical response which served as a reminder that originally carols were meant to be danced as well as sung."[2] Those taking part apparently experienced no inhibitions and the writer, who is a dignitary of the Church of England (Dean of York), seems to have had no reservations either. If justification for the practice is to be sought it will be found in the principle that the *whole* human personality needs to express itself in worship, a principle that has been accepted in the Catholic liturgy throughout.[3] In the Catholic liturgy at any rate the principle of the use of the body in worship has never been denied. Physical gestures like the sign of the cross, the genuflexion, bowing and kneeling have sometimes been regarded as so very Catholic that they were unacceptable to Christians of the Reformed tradition. Bodily movements have been strictly controlled, they are to be done in a particular way and to that extent they have become artforms. The same would have to be done about the liturgical dance. Any sort of bobbing up and down or waddling around would be undesirable because *unexpressive*, just as a bad celebrant who does not care about his bodily gestures is making a counter-sign rather than expressing the worship of the human personality.

Any extended use of the liturgical dance would of course arouse a good deal of opposition. People have all sorts of inhibitions and there would be those who would not and could

not take part in it. But then there are many who do not want
to sing or are unable to do so. They must be left in peace.
The liturgical dance, too, would be a relatively rare event
if only because it would need preparation and that takes
time, energy, and expertise. But if we are looking into the
future we must not rule out the possibility of the liturgical
dance. In many contexts the trend is towards a less formal
kind of liturgy, which however can still be dignified, and the
young are less inhibited about the use of their bodies than
their forefathers were. It may be added that the religious
dance is still part of the culture of certain peoples and there
is no reason why they should not be allowed to incorporate it
into their worship provided there is nothing superstitious in
it.[4] Here is a good example of how western Christians must
not try to impose their inhibitions and ways of acting on
others.

How, when, at what services, and at what part of what services, the dance is to be used are matters that can only be
discovered by experiment. What will be needed is a serious
consideration of the deeper meaning of the liturgy for, no
more than music, the dance must not be allowed to obscure
the real meaning of the eucharistic action. All the arts are at
the service of liturgy and the dance may not be an exception.

If however the dance frightens people, why not dramatise
the gospel? It is done with children and their parents watch
it with pleasure, not simply I think because their children
are performing. They feel that the message of the gospel
comes over more strongly. This too of course needs expertise
but not more than that required for a choir, or at least one
that is worthy of the name. It is likely too that the young
will be more suitable than the old and it might be something
to help them to see that worship is not passive or old-fashioned as many feel the "new" rite is. It will also mean that we
make a more intelligent use of space. Churches cluttered to
the limit with pews, benches or seats suggest, even now,
listening-boxes and Catholic people at least are strangely inhibited in moving in a church. The gospel could be broken
down into the different parts of the narrative and different
voices at different places could declaim those parts allocated
to them. If the passage is teaching (like the eight beatitudes) a

different treatment is necessary but still possible. Once again, there is nothing new in all this. The singing of the Passion on Palm Sunday and Good Friday was a dramatisation and when well done could be very effective. Even now, three readers with the choir/people forming the "crowd" make the Passion on these days something special that is appreciated by the people.

Music

Then there is the question of music. This for the non-musician—and perhaps for the musician—is a hornet's nest. The considerations that follow are however non-musical even if they have or, as I see it, should have certain musical consequences. The notion still seems to be about that a "Mass" say, "in honour" of St Euphemia of Antioch, consists of settings for *Kyrie, Gloria, Creed* (though this is now often omitted), *Sanctus* and *Agnus Dei*—all as if the structure of the Mass-liturgy had not changed at least in the sense that emphases are now put on different moments. In the General Instruction of the Roman Missal priority is given to the ministerial chants and the responses of the people that inevitably go with them. Among these the *Sanctus*, the acclamations, and the *Amen* after the doxology are the most important and with these is to be grouped the Lord's prayer which is the prayer of the whole assembly, president, ministers, and people. The *Gloria* has its role in the introductory rites and the Creed is the conclusion of the ministry of the word. The *Agnus Dei* accompanies the first part of the act of communion. The first thing then that needs to be kept in mind is the different roles that these texts variously perform in the celebration. For example, the *Agnus Dei* as the accompaniment to a certain action can be meditative in spirit and need not involve the vocal participation of the people. The Creed is an affirmation of belief, essentially that of the people, and it makes little sense if it is set to an elaborate chant that obscures its literary form and cannot be sung by the people. Increasingly it is felt that the Creed is best not sung.

Once the functions of the different texts has been seen, the next thing to do is to examine their literary form. The *Gloria* is a lyrical composition of which the first part is a series of joyful acclamations. Its literary form does *not* suggest a *durchkomponiert* treatment. The short phrases "We worship you, we give you thanks" can be dialogued between choir (cantor) and people or the melody could rise in a curve of excitement, from "We worship you" to "We praise you for your glory" where the people could join with the choir. The two supplicatory phrases that follow can obviously be quieter in tone and the conclusion as lively as possible. Perhaps it needs to be said that "active participation" does not mean that people give tongue throughout the Mass or even throughout a single text. That sort of method came into use, I think, through the Dialogue (said) Mass and it has imposed itself on many of the recent compositions that have signally failed to distinguish what are the literary forms of different texts and the literary patterns within a text.

Another peculiar notion that has been common in recent years is that "Masses for the people" must be unison compositions, one line melodies, and that repetitions of *any* kind are somehow "unliturgical". The shadow of Pius X's *Motu proprio* has hung heavy over church music for some long time. Repetitions are wrong whenever they distort the verbal text, when phrases are tossed back and forth for the sake of the music and to the detriment of the meaning: thus the old chestnut: *"genitum non factum, factum non genitum."* But if we *look* at the texts we shall see that sometimes they *demand* repetition. The most notable example is the *Sanctus* which is the joyful response of the people to the proclamation of the Good News of Salvation in the first part of the eucharistic prayer. Within limits the *Sanctus* itself could be repeated more than three times but where repetition seems to be demanded by the meaning of the word is the *Hosanna*. As I presume everyone knows, this is about the equivalent of Hurrah and everyone knows that a single Hurrah is bathetic. The same must be said of the *Amen* at the end of the doxology. Plainsong conditioned many of us to be satisfied with a little wriggle of notes at the end of a text doing duty for the affirmation that the word means. Where we have an *Amen* at the end of the doxology we have the people's affirmation and endorsement of the whole eucharistic action that has gone before. Here emphasis, gained by repetition, makes the people's response both possible and convincing. A threefold *Amen* seems to be necessary though it is conceivable that a slowly moving melody rising to a climax might also be satisfactory. The *Alleluias* before the gospel need to be treated in similar fashion. They are there to welcome Christ coming to the people in the gospel, are eminently a people's chant and must be such that the people can sing them.

What has been said above suggests that even the people's texts need not be restricted to dull unison melodies. The acclamations I have mentioned above with which I would put the response to the gospel and the dialogue before the preface can and I think should be richly textured. That is under the melody, sung by the people, there should be voices of three or four parts that will give resonance to the whole text, whatever it is. The Orthodox liturgy, whether in Greek, Ukrainian or Russian, has long used such a device and everyone knows how they compel attention and satisfy the soul.[5]

There are two more texts of the Mass that must engage the attention of composers, namely the responsorial psalm and the *Alleluias* and the verse before the gospel. The first plays a key role in linking the message of the first reading with that of the gospel and provides a means for the assembly to meditate on the word of God. No "Mass" in the sense of a musical text for the sung celebration of the eucharist should be regarded as complete without a setting for these texts. *Said* they can be dull indeed and according to the rules if the *Alleluia* is not sung it may be omitted. This is not just a rubric; it is an indication that it is essentially a sung text. Settings of these texts are already available and in places where the liturgy can be sung, settings of some interest have already appeared.[6] What needs to be done is to look at these texts and see what possibilities they hold for the future. The psalm stanzas belong to the choir, the responses to the people and if choirs wish to have music that stretches them—and many do—they will be better occupied with giving musical richness to the texts that belong to them. Musical texts of a rich texture, involving several voices, are a possibility and could reflect the mood of the psalm or the season (which in fact go together). For instance, the first responsory of Good Friday is, in the Christian interpretation of the psalms, the voice of Christ as he hung on the cross. That is the clue to an appropriate musical composition. The "Reproaches" are likewise the voice of Christ as he looks upon a world that has rejected him. Traditionally these have received musical treatment from composers like Palestrina and Victoria that are endlessly moving. They are best sung in the languages for which they were written (Latin and Greek) but the new musical texts should be treatments that are consonant with the English language. No doubt it will be a long time before Palestrinas and Victorias appear again but they will never appear unless efforts are made now.

The *Alleluias* demand musical texts that can be sung at once by the people and the choir who will support them and as with responses the choir can add the density of musical texture. If the musical form demands it, there is no reason why the *Alleluia* should not be repeated more than twice. The verse which belongs to the choir (or cantor) can receive a different kind of setting.

There is no doubt a good deal more that could be said but if we are looking to the future, and if we want a liturgy that is at once popular, i.e. within the capacity of an average congregation, and rich, the first and basic requirement will be to look at the structure of the Mass-liturgy, to examine the literary forms and functions within the liturgy of the different texts and then to clothe them with the appropriate music. As with everything else there are practical difficulties ranging from the statement that "The people do not want it", to the apathy of the clergy who are unwilling to do the necessary organisation to bring such singing into effect. For far too long we have suffered from, or been content with, a reduced liturgy and there is no reason why it should continue. Even if the gap between popular tastes and culture seems to be increasing, there is in fact a steady rise in the ability to appreciate good music and an even better teaching of it. If one may dream about the future, it is not beyond the bounds of possibility that with the use of good and appropriate music constantly used people will begin to learn to take part in singing in a way that has been customary with the Welsh, the Germans, the Austrians, the Ukrainians and others who for centuries have been able to break into parts when they are singing their community songs both sacred and profane. This ability is evidence of a true folk-culture that has been formative of European history and out of it have sometimes come the themes of the great classical music of more recent centuries.[7]

Whether the music called "folk" that is used often enough for "youth" Masses has a future is doubtful. It has been the fashion for some long time now and fashions among youth change quickly. Unless I am mistaken most of it *as music* is not impressive and it is doubtful whether it contains within itself the seeds of a future development that will deserve attention. It would seem to be more fruitful to look in the direction I have indicated above. That sort of music need not be conventional or in the Romantic tradition and it would be better if it were not. But if it is authentic it is likely to develop new forms as has the "classical" music of this century. There are signs that this is already known to current composers and some of them have given serious thought to the nature and structure of the liturgy. If they are allowed to work and that means that their compositions must be used *and paid for*, the future in this field is bright.[8]

The Defence of Human Values

There is another aspect of the matter that is not strictly liturgical. If the world is now entering a period of near-illiteracy and a disregard for what has conventionally been called culture, it would seem that the church has an obligation to uphold certain *human* values that are threatened. It has in fact been doing this for a long time now. The "social" encyclicals of the popes and more recently the Constitution on the Church in the Modern World have been concerned with the dignity of the human person, with the right to free speech and free assembly as well as with even more concrete matters like the morality of war and the protection of human life against abortion. Indeed the opening passage of the Constitution on the Church in the Modern World states that Christians are concerned with the whole of the human condition: "The joys and hopes, the griefs and the anxieties of this age, especially those who are poor or in any way afflicted, these too are the joys and hopes, the griefs and anxieties of the followers of Christ. Indeed *nothing genuinely human* fails to raise an echo in their hearts. For theirs is a community composed of men. United in Christ, they are led by the Holy Spirit in their journey to the kingdom and they have welcomed the news of salvation which is meant for every man. That is why this community realises that it is truly and intimately linked with mankind and its history." As the rest of the document shows all the concerns of the human race are the concerns of the church and while there are enormous social and moral problems, the document also states that science, culture and philosophy are part of her concern too: "Thanks to the experience of past ages, the progress of the sciences, and the treasures hidden in the various forms of human culture, the nature of man himself is more clearly revealed and new roads to truth are opened. These benefits profit the church, too, for from the beginning of her history, she has learned to express the message of Christ with the help of the ideas and terminology of various peoples, and has tried to clarify it with the wisdom of the philosophers, too."[9] Here is ample justification for Christians to care about the human values that are enshrined in language, the visual arts, music and movement; and if the world is to sink into a new barbarism, an indifference to language and a contempt for the finer expressions of human genius, let it be seen that in worship there is an oasis of sanity, a pool of calm and a window onto something that is greater than man and more permanent than the things which, however necessary for life, inevitably pass away. We can hope and wish for a liturgy which by an intelligent use of the values that are to be found in expressions of human genius will be an epiphany, a manifestation of the Mystery of God. If this is to happen then Christians will have to care for and probably defend the virtues of literacy, the importance and right use of words and the necessity of right thinking which the words will express. It will be necessary to show by word and example that worship is incompatible with the fake, the second-rate and the shoddy. Whatever is used in worship must bear the marks of the human thought that has gone to its making and, where appropriate, the marks of the hands that have made it. The reach-me-down objects acquired from an ecclesiastical furnishers should gradually disappear from our churches. Finally, it should not be thought that it is a matter of cultivating refined feelings for the aesthete. We are concerned with *human* values, values that are necessary for life if it is not to sink to a sub-human level. An inability to think correctly, an indifference to the ways we express what we think, a contentment with the debased in any form of art, bring nothing but the degradation of human nature and to that Christians cannot remain indifferent. As I see it, and on the assumption that the world is tending towards a new kind of barbarism, the church of the future will have to preserve and no doubt defend these values and reject all that is opposed to them. As in the Dark Ages, the church will have to educate, promote human talent wherever it is found, and save society from incoherence and chaos.

Nor should it be thought that the upholding of such values is a backstairs way of maintaining the purely literary and often cerebral values of the old academic humanism. Emphasis on those values led to the exclusion of others that were equally prominent and important in Renaissance humanism. The most conspicuous manifestations of that epoch were the creations of the visual arts, sculpture, painting and architecture. If a Florentine of the fifteenth century was conscious of a renaissance he was aware of it through his senses, through what he saw, through the changing buildings in which he worked and worshipped and, if he was lucky, lived. He could not read classical Latin and Greek though he may have admired the books in which they were written—if ever he saw one. The bookish humanism of a later time was the product, in England, of the schools and the universities which a young man could leave not only with no knowledge of art but with a contempt for it. The Renaissance attempted to form the *whole* man and in that it has been rarely followed. That it failed to do so is because it despised certain aspects of life that had been taught by the medieval philosophers who at their best upheld a vision of man that was both wider and deeper than that of the Renaissance. In our own day it seems to be the duty of the church to proclaim that vision again and to insist on the human values that are inherent in man but which are obscured by a civilisation that neglects or scorns them.

The Setting of the Liturgy

The title for this section is chosen deliberately. Churches exist and where they do they will continue to perform an important function in the pattern of re-organisation that is being suggested here. The parish church will be the focus of the smaller communities that make up the parish. The whole community will gather there for certain great events like confirmation and during Holy Week when the celebration of the liturgy demands the use of resources that do not exist in the smaller group. No doubt there will be other occasions too. The importance of such assemblies will be that they express in a way a small community cannot the significance of the local church. It will "represent the visible church constituted throughout the world" in a more adequate fashion than the small community (CL 42). It will be a fuller and more expressive sacrament-sign of the greater church. In the assemblies thus gathered the smaller groups will understand not just in a notional way that they are part of a larger community but really and at the level of life and action. If the diocese were small enough there would be an ever more significant manifestation of the church when the members of the diocese gather together for worship under the presidency of their bishop (CL 41).

However, at least in western Europe, the day of the conventional church building seems to be coming to an end. In many places there are too many churches already and the realisation is growing that even if new ones *can* be built, their maintenance imposes a heavy and continuing burden on the local community. Furthermore, it is being realised more clearly that a building that can only be used for a limited number of hours per week is an extravagance that is inappropriate in a world that, for all the technological progress, is getting poorer day by day. That suggests the final objection to church buildings that are inevitably expensive: are we justified in putting them up when in large areas of the world people are starving?

In any case, Christians have discovered needs that seem to have been largely unknown in the nineteenth century. There is a keener realisation that the eucharist, as well as the other sacraments, involve the *community* and while community can be expressed in a limited way in the liturgy it needs to be expressed in life as well. Christians who meet only in liturgical assemblies—and sometimes without wishing to acknowledge their fellow-Christians even there—are hardly likely to develop a social conscience. There is need then to provide places where the Christian community can meet for its own needs, the holding of parish councils, discussion groups, groups for the preparation of the Sunday liturgy, the organisation of the work necessary for the community to make its contribution to the life of the district in which it exists. But it may also provide for the needs of those who are not members of the church: rest rooms for the old, nurseries for young children, accommodation for youth groups and many other things as well. For all these needs what is required is a multipurpose building that can be both a place of worship and a social centre. There is nothing new in this. In many places such buildings already exist and are fulfilling their multipurpose function very well.[10] What now needs to be seen is that this will be the *normal* pattern for the future.

This is not the place however to discourse at length on the planning of such buildings. That is a complex and professional matter. Our concern must be with the "worship-space", however that is conceived. In the past dual purpose buildings have been or become drab in the extreme. As they suffered from dual use, the structure deteriorated and if there was a worship-space it was left as stark on Sundays as it was every day of the week. You could not but get the impression that you were worshipping in a building that was really intended for something else. This should no longer be necessary. Once people have got over the idea that church furniture and fittings have to be fixed (and therefore unsuitable for a multipurpose building) and once it is seen that there is a possibility of creating worship space with objects that are mobile and can be changed from time to time, it will also be seen that an atmosphere suitable for worship can be created. Textiles, pictures, even statues, can be put in place when necessary and can be varied according to the feasts and seasons of the year, as has been suggested for the conventional church. If this were done it would gradually lessen the different between the two kinds of buildings.

Even the larger pieces of church furniture like altars, lectern and fonts can be mobile and the altar could be placed wherever it was most convenient for the kind of assembly, large or small, gathered for worship. As long as the space is uncluttered the interior arrangements can be as flexible as you please. As for lighting this should be as flexible as possible so that those places can receive it as and when required. Seating continues to be a problem and it would be well to have less rather than more. Perhaps the children could sit on the floor as they do quite naturally in house-Masses and other small groups.

For the eucharistic communities mentioned above it would seem that some modest accommodation will be necessary. This could be a room attached to the priest's house and for non-worship occasions would be simple and furnished only in view of the purposes it is going to serve: discussion, the planning of work, the necessary meetings of helpers and so on. But for the Sunday eucharist it too could be decorated with tapestries on the wall, textiles on altar and lectern, a religious picture or something similar. None of these things need be expensive and many if not most could be made by members of the community. This sort of "active participation" has always been valued and usually enjoyed by the people.

Where churches already exist and need re-ordering this calls for the highest kind of professional skill. Merely planting an altar "facing the people" (which of course it does not; the celebrant does) in some place decided on by the parish priest may produce a nonsense. The whole character of the building must be considered and what is more important, the whole purpose of the liturgy that is to be celebrated in it. A new place for the altar may be of little benefit for those sitting some thirty rows back. The building may need to be turned side-on if the people are to be able to meet as a community and feel they are a community. However, it may be admitted that there are many problems here and it is important to say that there is no one overall solution to problems that are different in almost every church. What one would ask for however is that while the demands of different buildings are respected, there should be a willingness to create with light, space, colour, moveable objects, pictures, statues or other visual images which of themselves will create the right ambiance for worship according to the Roman rite. Dreary neo-Gothic buildings can be transformed by the use of such media.

9 The Eucharist and Other Sacraments

One of the virtues of the Constitution on the Liturgy is that it makes clear that the celebration of the sacraments is an integral part of the liturgy. It was not always so and even in the earlier decades of the liturgical movement the sacraments, other than the eucharist, rarely if ever were thought to deserve mention. They were seen as somewhat disconnected elements of the Christian life that had little if anything to do with worship. Even St Thomas's teaching that the sacraments are both for the good of man *and* the worship of God was disregarded.[1] This is so because when we approach the sacraments we profess our faith and acknowledge our complete dependence on God and that is worship.[2] Nor was their connection with the eucharist clearly seen. The organic relationship of the sacraments of initiation to the eucharist was simply forgotten. Baptism, confirmation and the eucharist, all as so many phases of a single liturgical action was, for long, the picture Christians had in their minds of those sacraments, and when St Thomas stated that all the sacraments were "ordered" to the eucharist he was saying in a more intellectual way what the church had been living for centuries. Before the liturgical reform of the last decade the only sacrament that *had* to be celebrated within the eucharist was holy orders. Now all the sacraments with the exception of penance, though with the inclusion of the anointing of the sick, may be celebrated within the eucharist. This is, of course, not always possible and in the case of the seriously ill not desirable. The new arrangement does however mark a great advance on the former situation.

When we come to consider certain of the sacraments it is not so much their liturgy that gives trouble but the pastoral situation in which they are celebrated. Baptism and confirmation are the two that offer most of the problems.

Baptism

As the pastoral situation is developing, at least in England, more and more children are not being baptised.[3] This immediately raises the question whether infants are to be baptised, when they are to be baptised, and how. The baptism of children with unsatisfactory Christian backgrounds is a matter of pastoral judgement which is rarely easy. If there is no discernible faith on the part of the parents the baptism must certainly be postponed and then should begin the effort to evangelise them, to win them back to the faith and some practice, however small, of the faith. It is not easy. If however there is some success, then the child may be baptised. But by this time he is probably of an age when he can, with the support of his parents, make choices and he must be allowed to choose whether to be baptised or not. Great damage has been done in the past by rushing children of various sorts of converts into baptism without seeking their, the children's, consent.

On the supposition that the child to be baptised has reached the age of nine or ten we are then faced with the question as to how we should proceed. The Order for the Christian Initiation of Adults provides copious material for this eventuality (316-360), but unhappily it is not generally available even in the form given in the Order. This, as the document says, must be adapted to individual circumstances. In fact in no document of the liturgical reform is adaptation so strongly emphasised as here. Not only are the rites of the catechumenate which it envisages as preceding the initiation to be selected and used in the light of the needs of the occasion but the very texts of the sacramental rites themselves are to be translated or rather re-written to make them suitable to the child or children who are to be baptised. This is an important work, yet to be done, and priests, unless they have some special knowledge of children, will be hardly the right people to do it. A re-thinking of the texts and the right language in which the notions are to be expressed needs a special competence.

I do not propose to give a summary description of the rite

but will merely make one or two comments.[4]

1. Like adult initiation the rite requires a gradual approach: an enrolment, a (short) catechumenate, including instruction, baptism, confirmation (to be given normally by the minister of baptism and/or the priest who has had a hand in the initiation) and holy communion.

2. Considerable adaptation even of the rite will be necessary to meet different circumstances: e.g. a younger child will not need so long a process and the rites themselves will need simplification. But a response of faith should be secured.

3. For rather older children some of the subsidiary rites will need examination: e.g. the pre-baptismal anointing which may seem strange to a twelve-year old and the question of what sort of garment should be used after the baptism needs to be raised. An alb is all right for a boy. What about a teen-age girl?

What needs to be done, and quickly, is to get this whole rite drawn up in its main lines so that it may be used. The need for it is already with us. In the near future it will be more necessary.

With older teenagers use of the Order for the Christian Initiation of Adults will be used though this too may and should be adapted. The instruction could be extended over a certain period, as the Order suggests, perhaps during Lent, and the rites contained in it will form the pivots of the instruction. That too is intended. School contemporaries should be recruited to help the entrance of the youth into the Christian community and they will be his official sponsors at the liturgy of initiation. But the whole process should not be made heavy with an excess of talking and a minimum of activity and the event should be seen as a joyful one. The ideal time for the celebration would of course be the Easter Vigil and if this is not possible a Sunday when the event could be celebrated by the whole community.

The order of the sacraments of initiation will of course be kept, baptism, confirmation and holy communion. The celebrant or the priest who has instructed the candidate is empowered on these occasions to confirm.[5] It will probably be wiser to postpone instruction on the sacrament of penance until after the initiation and it seems sometimes to be forgotten that baptism remits *all* sins. If it is postponed, it will leave some necessary instruction to be given after the initiation and this is in the spirit of the Order that asks that there should be a more intensive spiritual life in the weeks that follow. That the approach to the church and to full practice within it should be gradual was the practice of the early church and is written into the Order. Too often in the past too much has been given at once with the inevitable spiritual indigestion.

It may be of course that the candidate would prefer something quieter and less public. Not all temperaments are geared to public celebration when they are the centre of attention. If so, his wishes should be respected though the presence of his family and friends should be regarded as indispensable.

Here then is a new situation that needs to be looked at and it should form a part of the pastoral thinking of the present time and preparation for the immediate future. In France since about 1960 there has been a full blown catechumenate and we should do well to consider our own situation. The possibility of the regular admission of adults into the church may seem remote in these islands but it may be on us before we have done the necessary thinking and planning. Much of the thinking has been done for us in the Order for Adult Initiation. We need to be in a position to adapt it to our own circumstances.

As for the rite of Infant Baptism it is to be hoped that in the future one or two changes will be made. The Renunciation of Evil is put with the Profession of Faith. The former would come more appropriately before the exorcism. The subject matter of the two is similar. There is even a case for putting the Profession of Faith there too as in the early church the renunciation was the negative part of commitment and the Profession of Faith the positive. To make clear that the parents' faith is engaged at the very moment of baptism the question, "Is it your will that N. should be baptised in the faith of the church which we have professed with you?" could remain where it is. It is to be hoped too that texts addressed to an unconscious infant (the enrolment, the giving of the white garment) will be re-phrased. The use or non-use of the oil of catechumens before the act of baptism has been left in the discretion of local conferences of bishops. Some at least have insisted on its use. It would have been better to leave it to the judgement of the parish clergy for they, and they alone, know the people with whom they are dealing and not everyone is enchanted with the smudges of oil now planted with some difficulty on the breast of the child. And what do you say about it by way of interpretation? The whole rite is a hang-over from the past and its future must be doubtful. If the baptism of infants is to take place with greater frequency within the Mass (and it is usually the only way to make it a truly festive occasion) the rite needs further simplification along the lines indicated for baptism at the Easter Vigil (28) when everything up to the exorcism is to be done before the liturgy of the Vigil begins.

Confirmation

All the ills from which confirmation has suffered have come from its separation from the other sacraments of initiation. It has become a sort of wandering liturgical Aramaean. With unwavering consistency the early church saw it as part of the process of Christian initiation and the order, baptism, confirmation and holy communion was never broken. The eastern churches retain to this day the practice of giving all three sacraments to infants in the one celebration. The Roman tradition, that is exclusive of Gallican or other influences of the later Middle Ages, has been equally consistent. Both in the Order of Adult Initiation and in that for Infant Baptism this teaching is retained though with some mitigation in the Order for Confirmation (11). Underlying this is a theology to the effect that confirmation is the completion of what is begun in baptism, a completion that can be expressed by saying that the Holy Spirit is given in baptism but established (i.e. his presence "confirmed") by confirmation. In all the early practice and writing on the matter in the church there is no suggestion of confirmation being the sacrament of "mission". But since the thirteenth century such a theology has developed and in recent years has been underpinned by statements in the Order of Confirmation and by material drawn from the New Testament.[6] This is not the place to contest this opinion. I will merely say that it is yet to be harmonised with early liturgical practice and writing on the subject. What however is more difficult to accept is that pastoral practice is making use of *both* theologies. Children are still being confirmed at about the age of eight or nine when a commitment to mission is hardly possible, and yet others of twelve, thirteen or fourteen are also being confirmed, sometimes at the same ceremony. In both cases confirmation is usually given *after* first communion, thus breaking up the ancient liturgical pattern.

In practice all this leads to the as yet inconclusive debate on the right age of confirmation and until the theological tangle is sorted out there seems to be no hope of solving the problem. If you take the first view, the right time for confirmation is before first communion at whatever age that is received. If you take the second view any age before twelve would seem to be contra-indicated. Whatever view prevails it is to be hoped that in the future the present ambiguity will be eliminated. If the first view prevails and if there is a desire for a rite of commitment at a later age, there would seem to be no reason why the church should not institute it. But it would not be a sacrament.

Penance

The first observation to be made about this sacrament is that it is the *only* one that at present may not be celebrated within the eucharist. Yet it would be quite possible to make arrangements for this and when services of penance are held it would seem the right thing to do, especially in Lent when many of the Mass-formulas are penitential. This requires however—and this is the second observation—that the present rules for general reconciliation and absolution would have to be made more flexible. The prospect at the moment is not promising. The theological question at issue is whether the individual confession of sins is part of the *ius divinum*. Yet already the situation created by the third rite of penance is a little confused. When penitents have been able to benefit from the use of this rite, they are undoubtedly absolved since they are allowed to go to communion immediately afterwards. What then is the *theological* force of the requirement to confess to a priest subsequently? It *looks* like an ecclesiastical law (which of course can be changed) which a penitent must obey to show his good faith and the genuineness of his repentance. But that is a matter of spiritual discipline.

The question has also been asked whether the prevalence of general reconciliation and absolution would lead to the abandonment of private confession. Perhaps it is this fear on the part of ecclesiastics that is limiting the use of the third rite. Such a fear seems exaggerated. So long as private confession is made available people in various crises of their lives, people in one or other sort of spiritual need, people who wish to unburden themselves of their sins, will seek comfort, guidance and absolution in private confession. There is no *rule* either in the Orthodox church or in the Anglican church but in both churches many Christians are happy to make their confession in private from time to time and according to need. In any case, such experience as is available shows that people who have been reconciled and absolved in the public service have willingly confessed their sins later. The psychology of the thing seems to be that once people have been relieved of their burden, they feel much more able to present their condition to the confessor. Perhaps the psychology of sinners has been overlooked! Then there are those who are inarticulate. For these the public rite is a boon and the chances are that *after* the service they may be able to say something more about their condition than they are able to manage at present. Another factor to be taken into account is the decrease in the number of pastoral priests. If this continues it is likely that the public reconciliation and absolution of penitents will become very common. [7]

Marriage

The pastoral problems connected with marriage are enormous and this is not the place to discuss them. There is however one matter that concerns the liturgy of marriage though it is fundamentally a pastoral matter. The liturgy of marriage is now rich and unmistakeably Christian. At least implicitly the couple are professing their faith throughout the rite. It implies a belief in Christ, in the church, of which marriage is a sacrament-sign, and in the Christian teaching on the sacrament. Is it tolerable that people who may have been baptised in infancy but who by the time they come to get married have no discernible faith, should be allowed to celebrate the sacrament with all its serious and life-long consequences? There is many a priest who is disturbed by this situation which he sees as a glaring example of inauthenticity in worship. There is a case for saying that "marriage in church" should be made more difficult than it is at present if we are to save the sacrament from devaluation and possibly sacrilege.

In the present Order of Marriage there is an anomaly. In the case of so-called mixed marriages it is permissible to have a wedding Mass but only the Catholic partner may communicate. It would seem reasonable that where the other partner is the member of a Christian church and has some belief in the eucharist, he or she should be allowed to communicate as well. On their wedding day the couple are drawn together by Christ, the marriage is the sacrament-sign of the union between Christ and his church, as the texts say, and yet a sign of dis-union is made. As long as the present rules are in force it would seem inadvisable to allow a wedding Mass in these circumstances.

The rite of marriage is now generally thought to be a good one. The one place where it needs improvement is the translation. "I ask you to state your intentions" sounds too much like a Victorian papa interviewing a suitor for the hand of his daughter. And surely someone can think up something better than "in good times and in bad" (second blessing)?

The Pastoral Care of the Sick and the Dying

The admirable series of rites, prayers, readings and gestures in the Order for the Pastoral Care of the Sick and Dying meets almost all the needs of the present. The principal weakness in the order for the anointing of the sick is the lack of all mention of the mentally ill and of what might be done for them. The introduction does indeed say that the anointing is for the healing of the *whole* personality and that its effects are both spiritual and bodily. This teaching may well justify the anointing of a person when the mental illness is having physical effects—as it so often does—but when it does not, it is more difficult to know what to do. Meanwhile psychological disorders seem to be on the increase and we can hardly expect that they will diminish. The modern way of living, the cause of so many mental disorders, is not likely to change in the forseeable future. It would be helpful to say the least to have a rite with appropriate readings and prayers combined with directives when and in what circumstances to use it so that the pastoral care of such people could be more effective than it can be at the moment. Co-operation with doctors, which is mentioned in the introduction, would become more necessary in these cases than is usual in those involving physical illnesses and although most priests have some acquaintance with psychiatry, we need to know a great deal more about it if we are to be able to judge when anointing is to be administered. Meanwhile we can go on using the order for the Visitation of the Sick which includes a laying-on of hands.

The order for the communion of the sick is much better than the old one but people who are chronically ill and are housebound, sometimes for years, long for the Mass. From time to time this can be celebrated in their homes but the present Mass-liturgy is too elaborate and too long. What one looks for is a rite that is really adapted to the situation. Its principal elements would be one reading *only*, some prayers of intercession which might be accompanied with the laying-on of hands, a short eucharistic prayer and communion. This would give people great consolation and would make it possible for priests to celebrate Mass in the homes of the sick much more often. Although officials of the church emphasise repeatedly the importance of the Mass, they apparently do not think through their own views. Catholic people, especially when they are ill, *want* the Mass and everything should be done to meet their desires.

The Dying and the Dead

If there are signs that the taboo on death is being broken— it is at least being discussed in public again—the taboo on dying remains. As we get older most of us continue to entertain the notion that we are immortal. The age of seventy comes and we do not *feel* very old, we come to the age of eighty and the future still seems almost limitless. We fall ill and doctors and relatives conspire to persuade us that we are *of course* going to get better. When we go to hospital the organisation for dying is so elaborate that the retention of an identity becomes very difficult and contact with relatives more and more remote. We die in a hospital ward *alone*.

There are difficulties of course in all this. At some point in a terminal illness, professional nursing becomes necessary and the patient is saved much pain and discomfort. It is a very delicate matter to tell anyone that he or she is going to die and those prepared to do it may lack sensitivity. The thought of recovery, as also the notion that whatever our age we are going to live quite some time, are expressions of the will-to-live that lies at the very heart of the personality. It can be an expression of Christian hope: we are in the hand of God, his providence is real, we can trust in his goodness, *he* will eventually do what is best for us. But we do not rise to such a state without preparation and the view that life is a preparation for death contains an age-old wisdom. If death is the final surrender of ourselves to God, the supreme affirmation of what we have been trying to do—and to give—throughout our lives, and if day by day we try to make that surrender to God, our death, whatever its circumstances, will remain the most positive act we have ever made.

What seems necessary then is a change of attitude rather than a change of liturgy. The provison made in the Order for the Anointing and Pastoral Care of the Sick is generous. It just needs to be used but it is difficult to use effectively if prevalent notions are allowed to dominate. It is curious that just as our entry into the Christian life by the sacraments of initiation is gradual so is our leaving of it. There is the communion of the sick which becomes a normal feature of life for the chronically ill or the housebound, there is the anointing which may also be given but which is usually indicated by some new turn in the illness, there is its possible repetition if there is another crisis, there is viaticum as death approaches and there is the commendation of the dying which carries the patient on to the moment of death. At one level, all these are *kairoi*, privileged moments of the movement of the Spirit in the soul of the patient, and, at another level, a Christian-psychological preparation that enables the patient gradually to face death and finally to surrender himself to God.

This I suggest is a new perspective that is too little known and that could transform the formidable phase of our life we call dying. Both priests and people need to accept some such view. The nexus between anointing and death has not yet been broken and it is disturbing that requests still come for the anointing of what is undoubtedly a corpse. The unhappily named "Last Sacraments", confession (if possible), anointing and communion, are too often administered in an atmosphere of crisis that militates against their proper spiritual use. Of course there *will* be times of crisis. No one, not even the doctors, can predict the incidence of a thrombosis. But so often nowadays illnesses, especially in old age, are prolonged and there is ample time for the process of leaving this life which, as suggested, can and should be based on the right administration of the sacramental and other acts.

It is another question whether Christians will be able to change the prevalent attitudes of doctors and nurses to make Christian dying in hospital or elsewhere a human act. We have lived into a post-Christian world and the medical profession as a whole seems to be less "pastoral" in its attitude to patients than it used to be. Doctors have become "scientists" and even technicians, and sometimes give the impression that the human personality is not of any great account. Here however we have an obligation to promote and uphold certain human values that also happen to be Christian ones. Scripture says somewhere that man's counsel is in his hand. That is, he is responsible for his own destiny, he is in control until consciouness ceases. Even dying he is a person with all the rights and dignity of a person. He is not a *corpus vile* for the manipulation of others however well-intentioned. He may *choose* to surrender himself consciously to God in death and he should be allowed to do so if he so wishes.

As for the pastoral care of the dying, what still needs to be done is to persuade relatives that in this matter they are the ministers of Christ. They are *there* and even when the patient is in hospital they will be able to visit him more frequently than anyone else. The priest will do whatever he can but usually he cannot be present for prolonged periods. Meanwhile the need for spiritual help continues. Quite certainly the *physical* care of the sick and dying is a work of love and mercy but Christians should be able to do more than that and yet, so often, they seem to be tongue-tied. The priest will recommend that the relatives should continue to pray with the dying after he has gone and will try by his example to show how it is to be done. But often he suspects that little enough is done. The Order for the Commendation of the Dying contains a considerable amount of material and valuable suggestions on their pastoral care, how to pray with them, what sort of texts to be used and the considerations that should be put before them. Their hope in Christ, who by dying overcame death, is to be strengthened, acceptance of their sufferings in union with Christ is to be suggested, and the anxiety which afflicts us all as we approach death, as far as possible, removed. Prayers may be longer or shorter according to the condition of the patient, familiar prayers to which he can respond in his mind should be said in a way he can hear them, brief comforting sentences from holy scripture (the Order provides a list), the signing of the patient with the cross, all these ways of helping the dying are suggested by the Order (139-140). It prefaces these suggestions with the staement that it is a matter of Christian charity that Christians should express their union with a dying brother or sister by praying with them and for them that they may experience the mercy of God and may have trust in Christ (138).

This material is unhappily not yet generally available and the most practical step to be taken is to see that it is. It needs to be edited intelligently, broken down in various sections and presented in usable form. If this is done, it will be possible to begin some practical catechesis on the matter.

The liturgy provided for Christian death seems to have met with general satisfaction. Much of the heavy load of doom and the threat of punishment has been removed and death is seen as a sharing in the passion and resurrection of Christ. But if the former rite concentrated on the last judgement and purgatorial pains, the way the new liturgy is used too often suggests premature canonisation. The vestments are white, there are glowing accounts of the deceased, which are often remote from the realities of his life, and an atmosphere of euphoria which may wound the feelings of the bereaved by its apparent heartlessness. Christian death is a celebration of the paschal mystery but that includes with resurrection both the passion and death. Christ himself passed through the agony of the cross before he reached resurrection with its glory and its joy. We cannot expect less and with the weight of our sins upon us we should expect more. Suffering and death, though transformed for the Christian by hope, are still an agony. It *is* the severance of the life of this world, the only life we have ever known, and since this life is good, its loss is a grief. We need to be more realistic about death—and life—and we need to be more sensitive to those who are bereaved. If due proportion is observed, hope is strengthened and consolation is given.

The custom seems to be growing that the homily which the documents say should be delivered within the funeral Mass is becoming the eulogy that the rubric says may be given before the final commendation. The purpose of the first is to expound the meaning of Christian death on the basis of the scripture passages that have been read or other texts of the liturgy. This may well receive concrete illustration from the life of the deceased—or it may not! Surely everyone knows that not all who die and whom we have to bury are paragons of virtue and there are times when the less said the better. The eulogy, if there is to be one, is best left in the hands of someone who knew the deceased well and, so, it will often be given by a lay person. Indeed, best of all, it can be left to a memorial service later on.

As for the future it seems that in urban areas cremation is likely to become the usual way of "the disposal of the remains". This will be a practice forced on us by the lack of land for burial. Now that the rules have been relaxed we should do well to think about the matter. We have come late into this field and inevitably had to accept a pattern that was laid down without consultation with us. What does not seem to be realised is that the rules, at least in England, are flexible enough to retain something of our own practice. A religious service at the crematorium is not a *sine qua non*. The body may be cremated and the ashes brought to the church for the Mass and other funeral rites. Even interment of the ashes in the church grounds is permissible and if this is done it means that the ancient pattern of Mass, commendation and committal, can take place on the same occasion. Where this is done it gives considerable satisfaction to the bereaved.[8]

However, if a cremation service has to take place—and there may be circumstances where it is necessary—there is no reason why we should not make up a service, compiled from the official texts, that will be suitable to the occasion. The message of the paschal mystery and of Christian hope can be conveyed and it would seem to be particularly important that it should be. But it has been pointed out that at a cremation service there is little for the mourners to *do*. Well, they can sing the hymn (or hymns) or respond to the prayers (both of which they often do rather badly). But it is suggested that candles might be used "to symbolise the light of Christ and the fire of the Holy Spirit who makes all things new". There is something to be said for this. The candles could be lighted before the committal part of the service begins and extinguished as the coffin disappears out of sight. Not all perhaps will welcome this. The bereaved are sometimes too stunned to be capable of direction and others may feel that the symbolism is too remote from their way of thinking. But it remains a possibility and we should remember that candles were used in the old rite and only practical difficulties, it would seem, have led to their disuse.[9]

Over the centuries the sacraments and their liturgy have undergone many vicissitudes. Their place in the Christian life has been depressed, they have been wrapped in a cocoon of canon law, they have been seen as disparate elements that had nothing in common save that they were "channels of grace". The importance of seeing them as organically related to the eucharist is that all of them celebrate and make present the mystery of Christ in his redeeming work. The sacraments of Christian initiation are a prolonged but very eloquent presentation of that mystery. The candidates are baptised in the death of Christ and rise with him by the power of his resurrection. As at his baptism the Holy Spirit came upon him, so does the same Spirit come upon them, both in baptism and confirmation. They take part in the supreme sacrament of redemption in the eucharist and receive the glorified Christ in holy communion. Penance is a celebration of the reconciliation that Christ brought about by his death and resurrection and makes it effective both for the community and the individual. Marriage in a special way is a celebration of the union that Christ by his sacrifice, offered in love, made between himself and the church. In ordination men are invested with a ministry which is at the service of Christ's priesthood and gives them some share in it. As priest and victim he brought about the paschal mystery and through his ministers this is made available to mankind here and now. In the sacraments of the sick, and especially in their anointing, the compassionate Christ who bore "our sicknesses and pains"[10] comes to them and makes effective in them the power of his death and resurrection: "the prayer of faith (in Christ) will raise him up."

If all this is kept in mind we shall see that the eucharist and the other sacraments are the celebration of the paschal mystery adapted to the main times, occasions, and needs of the Christian life. If it is not kept in mind, they will once again become devalued and will cease to animate the life of the body of Christ which is his church.

10 Prayer and the Community

Prayer, mental (declining), "devotions" (dying), the rosary (unpopular with the young), visits to the Blessed Sacrament (rare), Benediction (how often?), Months of Mary (?), Stations of the Cross (Lent, perhaps), all these and some other forms of worship and prayer have been practised by Catholic people in the last two or three hundred years, but their future seems to be very uncertain. There are those of course who blame the decline on "the changes in the liturgy" though in fact the gradual abandonment of certain devotional practices pre-dates the impact of the liturgy movement before Vatican II and anything else that has happened since. Evening Masses, that made any other form of evening service very difficult and often impossible, came as early as 1953 but long before that efforts to maintain Benediction and the devotions that usually went with it were proving to be vain. It was an almost universal complaint among the clergy that "you could not get people to come to Benediction". The truth is that long before the clergy had noticed it or were willing to admit it, the social situation had changed. In the old-fashioned urban parish the potential "audience" was all but immobile, there was little in the way of local entertainment and the tradition of the nineteenth century lasted into this. It was "respectable" to go to church on Sunday evening and anyway it broke its long monotony. Then in the 1930s the cheap motor-car became available and people began to move about as never before. There was the lure of the road which for the most part was still open, there was the teasing attraction of the country, hitherto only glimpsed out of the window of a railway train, and people went out. As the years went by there was the increasing mobility of the population from one part of the country to another and from one part of the city to another. The family group was broken up. With the break-up went the congregation for the evening service.

Whatever may have been the quality of the evening services (and it was often very poor) it did mean that a service other than the Mass was available to people. They were prayer-services that did something, at least, to nourish personal religion; at their best they helped people to interiorise what they believed and what the Mass celebrated. This was all the more necessary when the Mass was in Latin and was celebrated in so coldly objective a way that, apart from holy communion, it said little enough to too many. The evening service also offered the opportunity (often not taken) for a kind of preaching that was and is impossible on Sunday morning. It was possible to plan brief courses of sermons, especially for Lent. One could treat a book of the Bible or pursue a theme through part of the Bible. There were the saints to be talked about—and how little Catholics then or now know about the saints! All this, some of it good, much of it pious fustian, has gone and so far nothing has been put in its place.

Is it possible to forecast a change? One thing the clergy cannot do is to change the social habits of their people and they will be knocking their heads against a brick wall if they try to. But one thing both laity and clergy could do is to seek to get the law of the church on Sunday observance changed. At present, and for centuries, that law insists that the fundamental duty of worshipping God on Sundays must be an obligation to attend (note the word!) Mass even if the worshipper does not receive communion. But the worship of God is not restricted to eucharistic worship. If the words of the Constitution on the Liturgy mean anything then we worship God in a peculiarly significant fashion when we pray: "When the faithful pray together with the priest[1] in the approved form, then it is truly the voice of the Bride addressed to her Bridegroom; it is the very prayer which Christ, with his Body, offers to the Father" (84). This is a very high doctrine of public prayer but it remains nothing but doctrine unless it is put into practice. Let then the obligation to Sunday worship, which has its basis in the natural law, remain but let it be extended to forms of worship other than the eucharist if people so wish.[2] There are Catholics who for one reason or another do not wish to go to communion on a particular Sunday, there are others who cannot and there are yet others, Christians of other churches, who may wish to come to one of our services but do not like the idea of being present at Mass when they cannot communicate.

If this change were brought about there would be fewer Masses (and with the increasing shortage of priests this may come anyway) but the same number of services, which when they are prayer-services can be presided over by a lay person. At least one service a Sunday, the time to be fixed according to local needs and circumstances, would be a non-eucharistic service. It *need* not be in the evening, and perhaps better that it should not be, for Sunday evenings now seem to be largely given over to social occasions.

In view of such a change it is utopian to suggest that now that the church has a form of public prayer, available by language and content to everyone, the people will in fact pray it? No doubt there will be those who will mutter in corners "It is the Mass that matters" little realising that the aphorism was first uttered by a Protestant minister of the British government.[3] Unimpeachably true but not exclusively true. There are other things that matter as well. What, I believe, the clergy *can* do is to change minds. By our office we are "educators". Whether we realise it or not, every time we address the people we are trying to form their minds and often change their minds and if we are not trying to do that we had better shut up. It will be said that the *people* cannot use the psalms: they are too difficult. To that the answer is "Teach them". It will be said that the people do not "understand the Bible". An extraordinary statement when one remembers that the church in these islands is spending vast sums of money on schools and in England all but bankrupting itself in the process. Is it seriously contended that it is impossible to give the young who stay at school until they are sixteen and often later an adequate initiation into the meaning of the Bible? All these difficulties, if they exist, can be overcome if the clergy and pedagogues of various degree are persuaded that the public prayer of the church is "the very prayer which Christ, with his Body, offers to the Father".

There's the rub. We make proud professions and do nothing about them.

What then could be done? The first point to be made about the Prayer of the Church is that it should continue, not that large numbers should take part in it, though the more the better. Christ said "Where two or three are gathered together in my name I am there in their midst" (Mt 18:20). This remains true and if a few people gather together, preferably with their priest, and recite the Divine Office, they are praying the prayer of Christ. This is already being done in a few places (too few) and what is required is that it should be a general practice of the church. What is needed is a presence, a visible presence, of prayer in the church that manifests the church as the praying community of Christ. If such a gathering is not possible every day—though the Church of England has show that it is possible—public prayer could take place at least at week-ends. There is still the traditional confession hour on Saturdays and this could begin with or be preceded by Evening Prayer. If there is an evening Mass on Sundays (or Saturdays for that matter) the prayer could take place some little time before the Mass to make it possible for those taking part to retire before the Mass if they do not wish to attend it.

The General Introduction to the *Liturgy of the Hours* does in fact make it possible to combine Evening Prayer (or Morning Prayer for that matter) with the Mass. There may be a case for this, especially where a priest would otherwise have to recite the office almost always alone. But it has the weakness of *not* providing another kind of service at a different time and the amount of "wordage" if it is combined with the Mass is too much for a prayerful celebration.

There is however a more ambitious possibility. As we have said above, the number of Masses might well be fewer in the future and this situation will of itself reveal the need to provide other kinds of service. How often Evening Prayer, say, should take place must be a matter of local arrangement but some of the greater feasts would seem to be indicated. On these occasions an attempt might be made to make the prayer a real celebration with the use of lights, incense, vestments (cope) and song. Choir and organist will be required and may

be hard to come by but experience shows that when something is attempted there are people who will do what is
required. Some choirs, they say, are languishing for want of
something interesting to sing, and organists, at least in the
Catholic church, are few and far between because there is
usually not enough for them to do. Let the attempt then be
made and let us see what the results will be.

If such attempts are made it will be necessary to look at
the forms of prayer in the Divine Office. It does give the
impression at first sight of being rather complicated. There
are psalms and canticles, antiphons and responsaries, not to
mention hymns and readings. All except the last can be sung;
the question is whether it is desirable that they should be.
Psalms, according to the Oxford Concise Dictionary, are
songs sung to a harp. We may dispense with harps (though it
would be nice to use them) but agree that they should be
sung. More problems, the jeremiahs say, and of course there
are, but not insoluble. The number of psalms to be used for
Evening Prayer is not so very great and for pastoral reasons
their number can be reduced. One could use the same set of
psalms for several Sundays running or it is possible to sing
one or two and say the third. Antiphons which are difficult
to set for congregational singing because their texts are so
various, in fact lend themselves to an interesting musical
development. For this we should look to Orthodox practice.
I refer to the *Troparion* which is described as "a stanza of
religious poetry"[4] which is pretty well what the antiphon is,
at least at its best. Some of them, for Christmas and the
Presentation of the Lord, notably the *Adorna*, were originally
Greek and were imported from the East. If choirs want something to get their teeth into and if composers wish to get
away from eternally composing *Glorias*, these are the texts to
set. They could add a note of richness to the service and
could be listened to by the people. They would be meditative
moments in the course of the office.

There is a fair supply of hymns, though we need new ones,
and all that is required for responsories is a set of end-phrases
that will be easily repeatable. The canticles also offer interesting musical possibilities which are suggested by the way they
are laid out in the book. The most successful I have heard is a

setting in the Russian style by Margaret Daly of the canticle from *Colossians 1:15-20.*[5]

The reading, as is well known, may be lengthy and chosen from any part of the Bible. It will be best to take it in leisurely fashion, it will be followed by a silence and perhaps the celebrant will wish to base a homily on its content. This would mean that a style of preaching known to the Fathers of the Church would be brought back into use.

If a silence is observed, as is highly desirable, after the intercessions, it is possible to move almost imperceptibly into private prayer. The balance then between public (and choral) prayer and private, silent prayer is maintained.

All this may seem very grand and over-idealistic. Let us then return to our small eucharistic communities. Here of course everything will be simpler, indeed as simple as possible. The prayer will acquire a certain intimacy and warmth from being the prayer of a small community. It could be very calm, quiet, contemplative as is the prayer of the many small communities of religious scattered all over the world. The reading of the scriptures could become a true *lectio divina,* as it was for the first tiny communities of St Benedict. Returning from their work and withdrawing for a short time from the clamour of the world, members of the community would draw refreshment from the word of God they hear in the scriptures and strength from the knowledge that God hears them in their prayers.[6] It is my suspicion, not without some grounds, that there are many Christians who are looking for such pools of prayerful silence in an all too noisy world.

Mention should be made of the "Vigil" offices provided for Sunday, solemnities and feasts. They consist of three canticles and a gospel reading which for Advent is one of the resurrection accounts and for other feasts the gospel or some other passage appropriate to the feast being celebrated. It is to follow the Office of Readings (after the second lesson) and is concluded with the *Te Deum* and the collect of the day. There are two obstacles to its use. One is that the parish clergy at these times are usually very busy with the preparation of the feast, with confessions and so on. The second is that the texts are not available to the people unless, improbably, they possess a breviary. Its interest is that it provides another contemplative kind of office, usually with a note of joy, it brings into use a range of texts appropriate to the occasion that might not otherwise be used and it provides a pattern for an even longer vigil for those occasions (and they seem to be increasing) when people wish to pray throughout several hours of the night. Historically it is closely related to the office of the church of Jerusalem as described by Egeria towards the end of the fourth century.[7]

11 Liturgy and the Movement of the Spirit

I prefer to use the term "movement of the Spirit" rather than "The Charismatic Movement" because I have no wish to enter upon the discussion of that movement and my experience of it is too limited to give me any competence to do so. It is in any case too wide and too narrow for my purpose. Too wide because the Charismatic Movement in its concerns and manifestations goes beyond the liturgy, as of course it has every right to do. Unstructured or only very lightly structured charismatic prayer services can and do perform an important function in the life of the church. But *as it is usually thought of* it is too narrow for my purpose here. The Charismatic Movement has shown itself to be concerned with a particular kind of manifestation of the spirit, more personal and admitting a more direct experience than is usual in other forms of church life. But it needs to be said that the liturgy is itself a manifestation of the Spirit and the principal means in the church by which the Holy Spirit with his gifts is communicated. This may seem surprising to some, possibly because the presence of the Spirit was not prominent in the former liturgy, but also because the action of the Holy Spirit in the church and in individuals has been until recently largely ignored by western Christians.

It will be useful then to recall some of the significant moments of the liturgy when the Spirit is given. His presence and action are made plain over the whole range of the sacraments of initiation. At the Easter Vigil, when candidates are to be baptised, the celebrant plunges the lighted paschal candle into the water singing "We ask you, Father, with your Son to sent the Holy Spirit upon the waters of this font that all who are buried with Christ in the death of baptism may rise to newness of life." A less dramatic gesture is used in the blessing of the water for baptism "We ask you Father, with your Son to send the Holy Spirit. . ." and while the celebrant says these words he touches the water with his hand. In confirmation there is the laying-on of hands, the traditional gesture for conveying the Spirit, with the invocation of the Holy Spirit and prayers for the giving of his sevenfold gift. In the three additional eucharistic prayers there are epicleses of the Holy Spirit both before and after the consecration. The comprehensive nature of the action of the Spirit in the eucharist is made clearest in the fourth eucharistic prayer where we pray: "Look upon this sacrifice which you have given to your church and by your Holy Spirit gather all who share this bread and this cup into the one body of Christ, a living sacrifice of praise". Here the ascending movement of the eucharist, the offering, and the descending movement, the coming of the Spirit on the people gathering them into one body is made plain. As I have said elsewhere about the Hippolytus prayer (the basis of EP II): "This text sets out admirably the full meaning of epiclesis: we offer in the Spirit who comes to make us one through holy communion".[1] In fact it can be shown that the Holy Spirit is active throughout the whole eucharistic action.[2] There is hardly any need to mention that in the new formulas of the sacraments of penance and the anointing of the sick the action of the Holy Spirit has its due place. There can be no doubt that the liturgy as a whole and especially in its sacramental celebrations is a sign of the operation and presence of the Holy Spirit. What is more it is a sacrament-sign, that is efficacious, of the movement of the Spirit in the church.

While all this is true it seems that even now the structures of the liturgy are inhibiting the manifestations of the Spirit and sometimes the *manner* of celebration makes it impossible. The stream of words, which might be described as the stream of *unconsciousness*, that washes over the heads of the people is not conducive to the movement of the soul that it may make contact with and respond to the Holy Spirit who is given throughout the service. It is for this reason that the *silences* suggested by the new Order of Mass are important, silences after the readings and sermon, pauses in the Prayer of the Faithful, a pause for reflection after the consecration and elsewhere. The Holy Spirit can and does speak in the silence of the heart. There may be and usually are no manifestations, not even "feelings", but his action is certain. It is for this reason that the Mass or any other service should be celebrated as far as circumstances allow in an atmosphere of calm and recollection which, in spite of all the too well known difficulties, can be communicated by the celebrant. But it must be confessed that this is about all that can be achieved in the crowded circumstances of the urban church. We must look elsewhere.

Let us look at our eucharistic communities again. Here the atmosphere is more relaxed, the time factor will usually be of less importance, the style of celebration can be less formal and, as we have observed above, the sermon might well be of the discussion kind. It is in this context that at least certain gifts of the spirit can be manifested. Apart from those of healing or speaking with tongues (to which perhaps too much emphasis has been given in recent times), the gifts are many, various and "normal". There is the gift of faith which may mean bearing witness to the faith in the assembly, perhaps for the strengthening of the faith of others. This need not be a noisy proclamation but the quiet expression of a conviction of faith. There is the gift of *gnosis*, a deep penetrating insight into the faith once delivered to the saints. There is even the gift of *preaching* and none of these according to St Paul are the monopoly of the clergy. There are, as we know, many others too and St Paul sees them as gifts "distributed" throughout the body that is the *ecclesia*, that is the assembly. Here in the context of the small eucharistic group we should see the manifestation of the gifts as a *normal* part of worship. The presence of the Holy Spirit in the ministry of the word would become clear.[3]

Nor should it be forgotten that there are what might seem to be humbler gifts: administration (*diakonia*), giving, and even commiserating with those in distress and doing this in a way that communicates joy of heart (*Romans 12:6-8*). These gifts too will be manifested in the smaller group where those who "administer", i.e. look after the building, prepare for the liturgy and take charge of whatever material goods the community may have will be known to all. The "giving" will have a directness that is immediately obvious; it will be destined for the needs of the community, for those it cares for and for the support of the wider church. Consolation of the bereaved and of those who suffer whether in mind or body will be the sort of consolation given from a person to a person. And in all this the Spirit is present and manifested. Whether the community is to look for the gifts of healing or speaking in tongues (and St Paul says that then it will be necessary to have someone to interpret the tongues) is difficult to decide. All one can say is that the eucharistic community operating on these terms would provide the right atmosphere in which such gifts could "emerge".

No doubt there is now nothing new in all this. Charismatic groups all over the church have been meeting for some long time. But what might be new is that people should see that manifestations of the Spirit are not to be confined to special groups (with labels) but are part of the life of the whole church for whose benefit they are given. Liturgy and the movement of the Spirit will be seen to go together.

On the assumption that the Divine Office becomes in a future, near or far, the prayer of a great number of ordinary Christians, it will be seen this is a *kairos*, a privileged moment for the reception of the Spirit. St Benedict, who in the sixth century provided the office for all monastic families of the West, was perfectly well aware of this. Prayer, he said, should be pure and short "unless it chance to be *prolonged by the impulse and inspiration of divine grace*", that is by the Holy Spirit.[4] He thought of the calm and orderly celebration of the prayer as a quietening of the mind and the senses so that the monk could hear the voice of God in the psalms and in the readings and the Holy Spirit could make his presence known. That the revised office makes this possible can hardly be doubted, as I have indicated in the previous chapter. The antiphon may be followed by a silence or there may be one at the end of the psalm before the psalm-collect, if it is used. Silence is recommended after the readings in morning or evening prayer and, of course, it may be prolonged if the community so desires. But perhaps it is the intercessions that offer the most favourable opportunity for unstructured prayer when the official prayers have been said. There is no reason why the prayers of members of the community should not be uttered aloud. This may not suit all communities but where "charismatics" gather it would seem right that at least the first part of their prayer is structured and room left at this point for unstructured prayer. The community will have prayed the psalms "in the Spirit", they will have listened to the reading by which the Holy Spirit is communicated to them, and they will be prepared to respond to the movement of the Spirit. They will, in the words of St Paul, be praying "not only with the spirit but with the mind as well" (which he considered necessary) and the final result will be that the two forms of prayer, the liturgical and the charismatic, will be combined.

12 The End of the Beginning

Do we always remember that the eucharist is inexorably pointed on to the end: "As often as you do this, you proclaim the death of the Lord till he comes"? Yet when we look into the scriptures to see what they have to say about the *eschaton*, we find predictions of suffering, persecutions, all kinds of calamity. Jesus (in his people) will be in agony until the end of the world, said Pascal. Is it this that awaits us? May be, may be not. The interpretation of the apocalyptic literature is notoriously difficult and has attracted the lunatic from the first century until now. But perhaps it has this to say to us: though Christ promised that he would be with his church until the end of time, he never promised that that church would be a large and impressive organisation, that it would own great and impressive buildings, that it would exercise power even if that power were in the interests of the spiritual needs of its members or even of those who are not its members.

Does this mean that the church has to die a certain death— you proclaim the *death* of the Lord—until it can come to a resurrection that may take place in time but that it is destined to achieve when time ceases? Does it mean that the church must experience the *passio Christi* in its very body before it can show forth the light of the resurrection to mankind? If it does, then the church will act out on the stage of history what day by day it celebrates in the eucharist. In the words of St Augustine, the eucharist will become, in a new and highly conspicuous way, the *sacramentum* of the self-offering of Christ and the church will become what it offers, a victim in suffering that it may live more fully to Christ.[1] If the prospect is daunting, we have to say that all this is implied in the eucharist and is in fact the plain teaching of the gosepl: he who would save his life will lose it and he who would lose his life for Christ's sake will save it, for eternity. The martyrs knew it. An Ignatius, a Polycarp, Perpetua and Felicity offered themselves as living victims that they might save their lives—for Christ.

But martyrs were not just of long ago. Increasingly the church is facing regimes of the left or the right which inflict imprisonment, torture and death on those who resist them in the cause of human rights and justice to the oppressed. The iniquitous subtlety of modern government is that it first besmirches its victims' good name, then dehumanises them and, if it does not kill them, casts them on the rubbish heap. They are hardly impressive martyrs (they think) but they are martyrs all the same. This kind of attack is either preceded or followed by attacks on the institution. Church property is "nationalised", i.e. stolen, bishops are inhibited from performing their pastoral functions, priests are spied on and their sermons delated to authority. Even the confessional is not sacrosanct. Christian schools are abolished and all means of conveying the faith, except perhaps in the home (and only there with danger), are taken away.[2] With what seems a supreme cynicism, these authoritarian regimes leave the churches open: "going to church" can do no great harm! But this is not always so. Gradually they are closed and new ones made impossible.

With the material structure of the church demolished, and almost all its organisations gone, nothing of any consequence remains. At least so the persecutors think. But they are wrong. The people remain and the people are the church. They can survive and do. One of the most impressive features of our time is the survival of the Baptists in Soviet Russia. They have a deep conviction of faith in Christ, they have a very light organisation, they possess almost nothing, the Bible and whatever might be found in any house for the celebration of the Lord's Supper. They have been threatened, harried, beaten, imprisoned, tortured and dispersed. But still they survive, still they meet. The human spirit borne up by faith in Christ is unquenchable.

A similar phenomenon has been recorded among the

Russian Orthodox who indeed have an organised church which is forced to steer a very difficult course between fidelity to the gospel and the exorbitant requirements of the state. The church survives and continues to attract people, often young, to faith in Christ. But here another phenomenon has appeared. There have been certain quasi-schismatic groups who have severed their connection with the Orthodox church, they have gone underground and they have *not* survived. Yet others have gone underground and in one way or another have kept their links with their church and have survived.

In these bitter experiences of other Christians there is a lesson for us. I have spoken above of small communities, house communities. I have suggested that in and through them faith can be vitalised and nourished. It should be possible to see now that they are not merely desirable for one reason or another, to meet the needs people feel or to facilitate action, but that at the deepest they are the vital cells of the church's life. Here the church *lives*. If we are to look into the future, a future that may be hard and even dangerous, to a time when the church will be stripped, when conventional organisation will be impossible and all that we have thought necessary for the life of the church has gone, it is communities such as these that we should consider. They will be hardly identifiable as ecclesiastical institutions, they will, as I have suggested above, own nothing more than their neighbours and will be known, if they are known at all, as people who help others. The priest will be a working man, just like everyone else, married and with his family round him.[3] A community like this in these circumstances will celebrate the eucharist and live it with an intensity that is rarely known nowadays.

But what of the links with the wider church? These, it has been shown, are necessary if there is not to be doctrinal and other kinds of deviation. A small group however fervent cannot live to and by itself alone. The bishop is the indispensable link. He too would have to be a working man but his work would have to be of such sort as to leave him a good deal of liberty to move about. Mobility is likely to be the chief mark of his pastoral work. He will have to visit the groups assiduously, encouraging them, teaching them and keeping them informed of the affairs of the greater church. His sacramental ministry will be substantially that of any other priest except that he will confirm if necessary, though it is to be supposed that ordinary priests will confer that sacrament as a matter of course. Ordinations both to the episcopate and the priesthood pose particular difficulties in these circumstances but it is done and a successions of bishops is secured.

Links with the Apostolic See (wherever it may be) will be the most difficult to maintain though it is to be supposed that in future there will be a wide measure of devolution. In the Penal Days in England those links were maintained at a time when travel abroad and even correspondence were extremely difficult and often dangerous. In an earlier age of the church remote churches like that of Armenia were not in direct contact with Rome but with, say, the patriarchate of Antioch and yet they were conscious that they belonged to the *Una Catholica*. In different ages and in different places the organisation of the church has been different from that to which we have been accustomed in the West since the fourth century. Ireland, which had its own particular organisation of the monk-bishops, on the fringe of the declining Roman Empire remained fully Catholic even if there were one or two matters of discipline that caused friction. The church is one by a common faith and a mutal love among its members and by the love of all for Christ. If these are maintained the church exists and is in action. In these circumstances the eucharist, with its ministry of the word in which God's living word is proclaimed, and its ministry of the eucharist in which the union of faith and love is sacramentally effected, will be a lived and a life-giving experience and as the members of the community move out into a world that imposes suffering on them they will be conscious that they are living the passion of Christ in the hope of resurrection in him. They will be conscious that they are bearing the burden of their neighbours who without knowing it are carrying the agony of Jesus in their lives and hearts. If Jesus who is lifted up on the cross draws all men to himself, it is in this way that he will be lifted up again and again. But there will be no glory, no prestige, no acclaim from anyone. The glory will be obscured by the suffering.

Is this to suggest a *mystique de souffrance*, a passive attitude to a world that is unjust and oppressive, an individualistic kind of soul-saving? We are reminded of the agonising problem posed to the Christian who would struggle for social justice, who would oppose wickedness in high places and the oppression of the poor. Solutions are not easily come by. There are those who have taken the way of active resistance leading to violence. To many they have become heroes. But is this the right way, is it the way of Christ? It has brought other evils in its train and pragmatically it is difficult to find instances where violence opposed to violence has achieved its purpose. May it not be that the right way is *organised* opposition by such means as remain constitutional or at least in accordance with the inherent rights of man to freedom of speech and association? A government may suppress even this possibility, it will attack those who have part in it, bishops, priests and people, who will become visibly the victims of an unjust and oppressive state. This, at the moment of writing, seems to be the way the church in South Africa has taken. Their attempt may fail. Modern governments are almost irresistible once they are determined to oppress. But they will not last for ever and then the witness to Christ that Christians have borne will become like the seed that falls into the ground and seems to die but which produces much fruit.[4]

What is written above is in no way intended to provide solutions to problems to which no one seems to know the answer. Here if anywhere we must await the guidance of the Holy Spirit. Solutions, if there be any, will be found in faithfulness to God, in the scrutiny of the gospel message and in prayer but also in a willingness to make decisions whatever they may be. Even an apparently passive attitude must be a considered decision if it is to have the vitality to resist evil. Christ was apparently passive in the hands of his executioners but all the time he was offering himself for the salvation of the world. This attitude is central to the eucharist, to a eucharist that has to be lived out in the events of life and it may thus be central to a solution of the problem of how to resist evil. Make your living bodies, said St Paul, a holy sacrifice, pleasing to God (*Romans 12:1*). It is a case of translating into life what we celebrate in the eucharist. The "living bodies" are members of the one Body, Christ, and in offering with him the church becomes total eucharist.

It may be thought that the picture of the future I have been attempting to draw is too dark, that it is alarmist, fantastic, the product of a too melancholic temperament. Be it so, and it should not be thought that I look forward to any such future with equanimity. Among other things I remember the gospel warnings that faith will grow cold, that many will fall away from fear of what is to come upon them. But is it not equally unwise to *assume* that at worst everything will continue much as it is or to suppose that one day oppressive regimes will wither away, that the world will be converted, that the church will go from stength to strength and, in the supremely idiotic phrase of Dr Pangloss, all will be for the best in the best possible of worlds? There are no grounds for thinking so in our time and we have only our time to judge by. We may hope that things will be better, we must pray that they will be, for the salvation of millions of men and women will depend on what in fact happens. Meanwhile we are poised betwen the present and an unknown future and the time for decision is now.

It is one of the paradoxes of Christian eschatology that the "not yet" is already "now". The *krisis*, as St John so often said, is in the present moment; the decision we make and must make now is of eternal consequence. We decide for Christ day by day and if we think on the scale of human society it, too, is making its decision here and now. The present is pregnant with the future. For the Christian, human society is in a state of becoming and it is destined to be transformed. There will be a new heaven and a new earth and when this world has been completely incorporated into Christ, he will hand it over to his Father. Humbly, silently, the eucharist, celebrated by people of no importance to the world, is day by day reaching out to that consummation: "As often as you do this, you proclaim the death of the Lord till he comes". Through that eucharist, offered on altars and in the living bodies of people, the purpose of God for mankind is being worked out and the divine power that will transform the world is available and, we believe, effective here and now. The eucharist is the beginning of the end but the end is beginning now.

Notes

1. Once

1. It apparently did not occur to them that their own rubrics were imperfect.
2. *Storia Liturgica*, I, p. 281.
3. Four new prefaces were added between 1920 and 1955.
4. A further revision of the same psalter in a more conservative direction has been made and can be found in the *Liturgia Horarum* of 1971-2.
5. The only item I can think of that would present difficulties would be the Prayers of the Faithful which are obligatory, at least on Sundays.

2. The Future and the Liturgy

1. See *The Tablet*, 5 February, 1977, p. 136.

3. The Future of English

1. In the above extract I have slightly modernised the translation in the *Divine Office*, I Week of the Year, Monday. The translator, who puts "prayer" passages in the second person singular, is Maxwell Staniforth, Penguin Classics, 1968.
2. See C. Mohrmann, *Liturgical Latin*, E. T. pp. 53ff and p. 60 where she gives two samples of pre-Christian cult Latin.
3. For some considerations on this see *Christian Celebration: The Prayer of the Church* (1976), p. 12.

4. Literary Genres and their Future

1. It is true that the *Gloria* and the *Creed* were originally in Greek but in their Latin dress (which is ancient) they have harmonised well enough with the rest.
2. *Liturgical Latin*, E.T. 1959, p. 54. Miss Mohrmann thinks the people were carried along by the *"sens du sacré"* which they still retained. That of course is a factor that cannot be neglected.
3. See Lewis and Short, *A Latin Dictionary*, s.v. "oratio". Its use as "prayer" seems to date from the Christian era.
4. Cranmer's collects were successful because English in the sixteenth century was heavily Latinised.
5. Prayer for Thirtieth Sunday of the Year.
6. Prayer for Twenty-eighth Sunday.

7. See Thomas A. Krosnicki *Ancient Patterns in Modern Prayer*, 1973, Catholic University of America/Consortium Press, Washington, D.C.
8. It is another question whether these prayers are as good as they might be. They seem to be rather wordy not only to read but to use with children.
9. "How shall the heavenly Spirit come to the consecration of the divine mystery...?" Cf. J. A. Jungmann, *Missarum Sollemnia*, Fr. trans. III, p. 110, n. 37 who refers to *Ep. fragm.*, 7 (Thiel I, p. 486). He does not think it sufficient proof.
10. Cf. Mario Righetti, *Storia Liturgica*, III (1949), p. 384, PL, 65, c. 187: "When we ask for the coming of the Holy Spirit for the sanctification of the sacrifice of the whole church, in my view there remains nothing more to be asked than that by a spiritual grace (by the grace of the Holy Spirit) the unity of love in the body of Christ, which is the church, should be kept unbroken".
11. For texts see M. Righetti, op. cit. pp. 383-387. For the Mozarabic texts see Hänggi and Pahl, *Prex Eucharistica* (1968) pp. 500ff.
12. See John McKenna, *Eucharistic and Holy Spirit*, Mayhew-McCrimmon for the Alcuin Club, 1977, pp. 204-5.
13. Some of the new prefaces read more like petitions than proclamations with thanksgiving of God's saving works.
14. E.g. one of the Ethiopian prayers (Marian), *Prex. Euch.* pp. 160 ff, and possibly that of Addai and Mari, *ibid*. p. 377. For this view see E. Ratcliffe, *Liturgical Studies* (ed. Couratin and Tripp), (1976), pp. 87-88.
15. *Christian Celebration: The Mass*, p. 131.
16. This is the outlook of the Constitution of the Church in the Modern World.
17. *Prex euch.* p. 103.
18. The Syriac liturgies were, of course, nourished on the Syriac bible, the *Peshitta*.

5. Adaptation: The Way to the Future

1. They are sometimes crammed with disconnected ideas.
2. See *Christian Celebration: The Mass*, pp. 16-30.
3. It may be omitted if a local conference of bishops so ordains.
4. Tertullian, *De Baptismo*, 8. But see *De Resurrectione*, VIII, 3.
5. Even if it is not always possible to deliver a homily daily (though it is done in many places) it is not to be regarded as an optional extra. It is part of the whole rite as the Constitution and the missal say quite emphatically.
6. Apol. 67.
7. See A. G. Martimort, *L'Eglise en Priere*, p. 139.
8. See *Prex eucharistica*, ed. A. Hänggi and I. Pahl, pp. 495ff.
9. Some such scheme was before the Congregation for Worship some few years ago.

6. The Mass of the Future

1. Bruce Publishing Company, U.S.A.
2. *Notitiae*, January, 1977, 126, p. 29.
3. See R. H. Fuller, *Preaching the New Lectionary* (Liturgical Press, Minnesota, U.S.A., 1976), p. 482-6.

4. I am thinking here of the Sundays of the Year. The readings for the greater feasts and seasons do form a pattern and throw light on each other.
5. Decree on Ministry and Life of Priests, 2, 4.
6. On the Church, no. 12.
7. It was included in the draft of *Inter oecumenici* of 1964.
8. Janvier, 1977, p. 78.
9. Mayhew-McCrimmon, 1976.
10. The above samples are to be found in *Communautes et Liturgies*, Janvier, 1977, pp. 77-81. They are by N. Berthet and R. Gantoy.
11. For the story, see C. Howell, *Clergy Review*, February, 1977, p. 59, n. 2.
12. It has been dropped from *Series III*.
13. See J. A. Jungmann, *Missarum Sollemnia*, Fr. T., III, p. 119 and n. 4. A. Fortescue, *The Lesser Eastern Churches* (1913) pp. 284-5.
14. See L. Ligier "From the Last Supper to the Eucharist" in *The New Liturgy* (ed. L. Sheppard, 1970, pp. 113ff.)
15. In the Northampton diocese the lay-ministers take communion to the sick on Sundays after Mass, a day when the clergy can hardly do so.
16. To say that the consecration is for the communion of the *priest* is to revert to a kind of hieraticism that is unacceptable today. The priest's communion does in fact preserve the *validity* of the action but no more.

7. The Community

1. See M. M. Winter *Mission or Maintenance* (1973), pp. 58-9.
2. Cf. *A Time for Building*.
3. Some years ago a whole conference of bishops in Africa made the proposition and interestingly enough one of their conditions was that the man chosen must be from the local community and acceptable to it.
4. In France the collaboration of the worker-priest with the parish clergy is known to have increased the effectiveness of the latter's work.
5. The full text is to be found in *Briefing* (7 May, vol. 7, no. 15; 74 Gallows Hill Lane, Abbots Langley, Herts) from which the extracts are taken.

8. The Presentation of the Liturgy

1. R. C. D. Jasper "Worship and Dance Today: A Survey", p. 23, in *Worship and Dance*, ed. J. G. Davies, Institute for the Study of Worship and Religious Architecture, Birmigham University, 1975.
2. Op. cit. p. 25.
3. See *Worship and Dance* where Professor Davies gives a history of the dance in liturgy from the fourth to about the seventeenth century, pp. 16-19 (though it must be said that the church authorities more often than not tried to suppress it) and pp. 43-56 where he sketches out a theology of the liturgical dance.
4. See Constitution on the Liturgy, 37-40.
5. See also the setting of the Colossians canticle for Vespers by Margaret Daly, Institute for Pastoral Liturgy, Portlaoise, Ireland.

6. The Society of St Gregory has to its credit a number of such settings, some it is true rather difficult, that have been written for and sung at successive summer schools.
7. I am told that the melody of *O Sacred Head*, turned by Bach into his famous chorale, was originally·in the Middle Ages a love song.
8. Among the names that come to mind are Anthony Milner, Bill Tamblyn, Christopher Walker, though of course there are others.
9. No. 44. *Documents of Vatican II*, Abbott and Gallagher (London-Dublin, 1966) p. 246.
10. Examples can be found in the various publications of the Birmingham Institute for Worship.

9. The Eucharist and Other Sacraments

1. Cf. CL 59 and *Summa Theologica* III, 63, 1.
2. Cf. *Christian Celebration: The Sacraments* (1973) p. 4.
3. Recent pastoral visitation in my parish has revealed in a matter of days three children unbaptised, one 10, one 5, and a third 3. More recently still I baptised three, 10, 8 and 1, of another family.
4. See *Christian Celebration: The Sacraments*, pp. 58-60.
5. Order for the Christian Initiation of Adults, 228.
6. Order, 2. Cf. A. P. Milner, *The Theology of Confirmation*, Cork, 1972, pp. 90-99.
7. For further consideration of this matter see Brian Newns, "General Absolution and Recent Trends" in *Clergy Review*, January 1977, pp. 62-68 and *ibid*. Joseph McMahon "Confession — Is there any hope?" pp. 60-62.
8. An answer in *Notitiae* (Jan. 1977, 45) rejects the view and the practice suggested above. Its main argument is that the ashes do not represent the *body* of the deceased and it is this that receives the honour given in the funeral rite because it was the temple of the Holy Spirit. The statement bases itself on the authenticity of signs. But even Tertullian says somewhere that a corpse has no category; you cannot really say what it is and for most people the ashes are as much the remains of the deceased as the corpse. And what should be done with an exhumed body, buried for years and now dust, that has never received Christian burial? However if the above reply is to be regarded as obligatory, my suggestion cannot be used. Further discussion would be helpful.
9. Or perhaps because there is no rubric *ordering* their use people have thought that the custom was abrogated!
10. *Isaiah 53:4-5* (RSV, margin).

10. Prayer and the Community

1. And we may say "without him" if he cannot be there or is not there.
2. It is to be hoped too that the obligation to attend Mass "under the pain of mortal sin" will be removed. No one believes in it now.
3. Augustine Birrell, sometime Chief Secretary for Ireland.
4. *The Festal Menaion* (Service Books of the Orthodox Church, trans. Mother Mary and Archimandrite Kallistos Ware, 1969), p. 561, Glossary, s.v.

5. Institute for Pastoral Liturgy, Portlaoise, Ireland.
6. This is the sentiment of St Augustine describing his mother's prayer when she went daily to church for the office. See *Christian Celebration: The Prayer of the Church* (1976), p. 39.
7. See *Christian Celebration: The Prayer of the Church*, p. 39.

11. Liturgy and the Movement of the Spirit

1. "The Holy Spirit in the Eucharistic Celebration" in *Pastoral Liturgy*, ed. H. E. Winstone (1975), p. 27.
2. *Art. cit.* pp. 19-29.
3. For scripture references see *I Cor. 12:4-11; 13:8-12; 14* where St Paul is concerned for harmony and good order in the assembly.
4. *Rule*, chapter 20 (ed. and trans. Abbot Justin McCann, 1972), p. 69. Cf. also chapter 52, p. 119.

12. The End of the Beginning

1. Cf. *De Civitate Dei*, X, 6 and 20.
2. Even in England few seem to realise that a government take-over of *all* schools would provide the best possible means for ensuring that children will never learn anything but what those in power think fit they should know. This now is perhaps the strongest case for the Christian school.
3. Where was it that I read that amazing account of a distinguished Russian surgeon, thought by everyone to be a member of the Party, who when he came to die was revealed to be an archbishop?
4. Whether the Jesuit priests and lay-brother and the Dominican nuns who were murdered in Rhodesia in 1977 were martyrs is doubtful but their lives beforehand and the forgiving attitude of their colleagues since are a witness in which, one suspects and hopes, lie the seeds of reconciliation.